OVERCOMING THE
ENEMY

BY

CHARLES F. STANLEY

THOMAS NELSON
Since 1798

Contents

Contents

Preparing to Overcome the Enemy

The world today believes that the devil does not exist. It believes that he is merely an ancient myth, a metaphor to explain the presence of evil in our world. But the Bible teaches clearly that the devil is very real, and he hates you very much.

That's the bad news. The good news is that Jesus Christ has already defeated the devil—utterly, permanently, and irrevocably. That does not mean that you will never be confronted by the enemy of your soul; on the contrary, he is still actively seeking your harm. But the power of Jesus Christ is all you need to defeat the devil every time he attacks.

This book can be used by you alone or by several people in a small-group study. At various times, you will be asked to relate to the material in one of these four ways:

1. *What new insights have you gained?* Make notes about the insights that you have. You may want to record them in your Bible or in a separate journal. As you reflect back over your insights, you are likely to see how God has moved in your life.

2. *Have you ever had a similar experience?* Each of us approaches the Bible from a unique background—our own particular set of relationships and experiences. Our experiences do not make the Bible true—the Word of God is truth regardless of our opinion about it. It is important, however, to share our experiences in order to see how God's truth can be applied to human lives.

3. *How do you feel about the material presented?* Emotional responses do not give validity to the Scriptures, nor should we trust our emotions as a gauge for our faith. In small-group Bible study, however, it is good for participants to express their emotions. The Holy Spirit often communicates with us through this unspoken language.

4. *In what way do you feel challenged to respond or to act?* God's Word may cause you to feel inspired or challenged to change something in your life. Take the challenge seriously and find ways of acting upon it. If God reveals to you a particular need that He wants *you* to address, take that as "marching orders" from God. God is expecting you to *do* something with the challenge that He has just given you.

Start and conclude your Bible study sessions in prayer. Ask God to give you spiritual eyes to see and spiritual ears to hear. As you conclude your study, ask the Lord to seal what you have learned so that you will never forget it. Ask Him to help you grow into the fullness of the stature of Christ Jesus.

Again, I caution you to keep the Bible at the center of your study. A genuine Bible study stays focused on God's Word and promotes a growing faith and a closer walk with the Holy Spirit in *each* person who participates.

Lesson 1

Our Foremost Enemy

--- ❧ **In This Lesson** ❧ ---

LEARNING: IS THE DEVIL REAL?

GROWING: WHO WOULD WANT TO HARM ME SPIRITUALLY?

Believers in Christ Jesus have three main enemies in life. They are constantly present to harass us, create conflict for us, and generate trouble for us. We cannot escape any of them completely as long as we live, although we are assured of victory over them as long as we rely on the Lord Jesus for our wisdom, power, and ability to endure. Our three enemies are:

1. The world. The world includes anything of a physical nature that might hinder us in our walk with Christ or might tempt us to sin. Contrary to what some people think, the world is not getting better. If anything, it's getting worse because so many more possibilities for evil exist today than hundreds or thousands of years ago: the world has more people, greater opportunities for evil alliances and evil behavior, more technology for delivering tempting messages, more information about how to engage in evil, and more varieties of false religions. The ways and means for committing evil have exploded, not diminished.

2. The flesh. The nature of the human heart has not changed since the creation of man. The human heart still has a bent toward darkness, evil, and sin. We have desires which God wants us to meet in ways that are in keeping with His commandments. The temptation always exists, however, for us to meet those desires in ways that are ungodly. We never lose our human, fleshly desires, and we never lose our capacity to yield to temptation. These desires are with us until we die because they reside within us.

3. The devil. Peter describes our enemy this way:

> Your adversary the devil walks about like a roaring lion, seek-ing whom he may devour.
>
> —1 Peter 5:8

Each of us faces a spiritual battle with the devil today, whether we re-alize it or not. The very nature of the enemy is to defeat us, destroy us, and to kill everything that is important to us. His pursuit of us is persistent, unrelenting, and always aimed at the most vulnerable area of our lives.

Why does Peter describe the devil as "your adversary"? Why does he compare him to a "roaring lion"?

Why do some people think the devil does not exist? What do *you* think? What does the Bible teach?

A Need for Daily Victory

These three enemies are always with us, and our best recourse is to learn how to deal with them and how to have daily victory over them. It would be wonderful if we could go on a fasting and prayer retreat to defeat the enemies once and for all in our lives, but that isn't a provision God has made for us. Rather, He has provided us with the Holy Spirit who resides within us to help us in our struggle. The Holy Spirit gives us the ability to say no to the temptations of the world and to overcome and control our fleshly desires. The Holy Spirit also enables us to withstand the assaults of the devil on a day-to-day basis and to experience peace and wholeness even in the face of severe spiritual opposition.

We face a daily struggle, but we can also experience daily victories. Our Lord calls us to live one day at a time. We will not have a single, definitive showdown with the devil in our lives—a moment in which he is defeated and made unable to accuse or torment us again—but we can experience a *daily* victory over the devil. We can say no to the temptations he presents *today*. We can use our faith to defeat his assault against our minds, bodies, and spirits *today*. We can pray against his efforts to destroy us *today*. A string of daily victories makes a victorious life!

> For the flesh lusts against the Spirit, and the Spirit against the flesh; and these are contrary to one another, so that you do not do the things that you wish.
>
> —Galatians 5:17

⋙ What does it mean that "the flesh lusts against the Spirit"? Give some practical examples of this.

➣ In what sense is the Spirit contrary to the flesh? Why must a Christian deny one—flesh or Spirit—in order to indulge the other?

Focusing on Our Spiritual Battle

We battle against the world and the flesh by learning first how to discern God's will in a given situation and then how to have the courage to say no to evil. These battles are won or lost primarily on the battleground of our physical, material, and emotional lives.

This study recognizes that we are engaged in an ongoing battle to overcome the world and the flesh, but it is based on the premise that the devil is behind these battles. Ultimately, our battle in each of these areas is spiritual in nature. It is waged in the spirit, and it has eternal and far-reaching spiritual consequences.

The devil's purpose is not simply to irritate us or make our lives difficult. His goal is to destroy us in the spirit realm. The devil will use whatever is made available to him as a toehold on which to establish his evil purposes. His ultimate goal is to annihilate us—physically, materially, emotionally, mentally, and spiritually.

An Assurance of Victory

As we focus on spiritual warfare, we will do so from the perspective that the devil is a defeated foe. We cannot defeat him by our own authority; rather, he has been defeated by Jesus Christ. Jesus referred to the devil as the "ruler of this world" (John 12:31), and He said of him, "he has nothing in Me" (John 14:30). The devil has no authority, power, or influence over Jesus. The book of Revelation graphically details Jesus' definitive victory over the devil when He casts him "into the lake of fire and brimstone" where the devil "will be tormented day and night forever and ever" (Rev. 20:10).

You may ask, "If the devil is a defeated foe, why do we still have to fight?" The victory over the devil is assured in reality, but it is not yet accomplished in time. The fate of the devil is sealed, but he will have access to mankind until the day when God brings this age to an end. The existence of the devil is related to our having free will as human beings. God has given human beings the ability to choose, and that includes our ability to choose evil. The devil, as the supreme agent of evil, has the power to tempt us and to oppress us.

What we do know with certainty is that *any* time the devil is confronted with Jesus, Jesus wins. When we place our faith and hope in Christ and resist the devil, the devil cannot score a victory over our lives. We may lose battles against the devil from time to time, but *we will not lose the war* because we belong to Christ.

It is important to keep this assurance of victory at the forefront of our thinking as we study spiritual warfare. If we look only at the devil and his tactics, it is easy to become discouraged or fearful. If we keep our focus on Jesus Christ, however, we remain strong and alive in our spirits.

Do not love the world or the things in the world. If anyone loves the world, the love of the Father is not in him.

—1 John 2:15

❧ What does it mean to love the world?

❧ Why is love of the world incompatible with love of God?

The Great Value of Christian Allies

Everyone faces spiritual battles, and every person knows what it means to come up against the devil's assaults. This is an area in our Christian walk in which each of us should have great empathy toward our brothers and sisters in Christ. One of our greatest privileges and responsibilities is to help our fellow believers fight and win spiritual battles. No person is intended to confront the devil alone. Christ assures us that He is always present. Even so, we are to function as the *body* of Christ, one to another. We are to join forces with those who are under attack by the enemy and become fellow warriors, doing battle in the spirit realm through our prayers and loving support.

As you face spiritual battles, you are wise to turn to your brothers and sisters in Christ and ask for their help. As you see others facing spiritual battles, you are admonished by the Scriptures to go to them and help them win a victory through Christ Jesus. We are to fight against our common enemy, Satan, and his demons. Imagine how much would be accomplished in our churches today if believers would band together against their true enemy, rather than wasting their time and energy bickering with one another or fighting against matters of lesser importance.

I encourage you to see your Bible-study group as a band of God's warriors, powerfully equipped for battle through your relationship with Christ Jesus and your empowerment by the Holy Spirit. Expect your study of the Word to equip you to help one another as you continue to build your relationship with other believers in your church or community after your study has ended.

ᔑ Today and Tomorrow ᔑ

TODAY: THE DEVIL IS VERY REAL, BUT JESUS HAS UTTERLY DEFEATED HIM.

TOMORROW: I WILL ASK THE LORD TO HELP ME SEE WHERE I CAN STRENGTHEN MY SPIRITUAL LIFE THIS WEEK.

Lesson 2

The Nature of Our Enemy

---------- ✍ In This Lesson ✍ ----------

LEARNING: JUST WHO IS THE DEVIL?

GROWING: WHAT CAN THE DEVIL DO TO ME?

One of the foremost rules of warfare is to know your enemy. The more you know about your enemy—how he thinks, what motivates him—the more likely you are to defeat him. To overcome the enemy of our eternal spirit, the first thing we must know about him is his nature.

Peter described the devil as a "roaring lion, seeking whom he may devour" (1 Peter 5:8). Most big-game hunters consider the lion the most dangerous of animals. It is extremely powerful and can move very fast and very low (out of sight in tall grassland areas). It has a great ability to track its prey, being stealthy in its maneuvers and deceptive in its motives. A lion's awesome roar instills fear that often paralyzes its prey, making conquest all the easier.

Peter accurately identified all of these characteristics with the devil. The devil is powerful, deceptive, and secretive, and he can act swiftly if given an opportunity. His roar against us can cause us to quake in fear. Peter was writing to Christians who were enduring great persecution, and they readily understood this graphic image. The enemies of Christianity often operated secretly. The early Christians knew they had enemies waiting to pounce on them for their faith, but the enemies' identity was often unknown to the Christians.

Peter also said that the devil shows no favoritism when he attacks: "The same sufferings are experienced by your brotherhood in the world" (1 Peter 5:9). The devil acts like a roaring lion toward believers and unbelievers alike. His behavior doesn't change according to his prey; it is his *nature* to be like a roaring lion, seeking whom he may devour. A lion's actions are consistent, whether its prey is a wildebeest or a young zebra. A lion always acts like a lion.

The devil is often depicted humorously as a little imp with a pitchfork sitting on a person's shoulder and whispering naughty things into his ear. Nothing could be farther from the truth. The devil is always seeking our destruction. He is forever on the prowl, never satisfied with his most recent kill. It is his nature to destroy, to kill, to maim, to devastate. Jesus said that the devil comes at us with the purposes of stealing anything of value, killing our relationships, and destroying our health and our lives (John 10:10).

The devil is a fierce opponent, a deadly enemy. There is nothing humorous about his tactics or his intent, and there certainly is nothing to laugh about if you are his intended victim. We do ourselves a serious disservice if we discount his existence, take him lightly, or believe that we are capable of defeating him in our own strength.

> He [the devil] was a murderer from the beginning, and does not stand in the truth, because there is no truth in him. When he speaks a lie, he speaks from his own resources, for he is a liar and the father of it.
>
> —John 8:44

☙ What characteristics does Jesus reveal about the devil in this verse?

☙ How do these character traits differ from the world's views of the devil?

Other Descriptions of the Enemy

Peter called the devil an "adversary" (1 Peter 5:8), someone who opposes you. An adversary may oppose what you say or do, or he may be hostile toward you simply because you exist. A real enemy is someone who dislikes you simply because you were born. An adversary will take a stand against you no matter what you do or don't do. His goal is to defeat you because he wants to defeat you. He takes personal pleasure in doing so.

This means that we don't have to *do* anything to earn the devil's disapproval and hatred. Certainly, there's nothing we can do to earn the devil's approval! He is opposed even to those who give in to him and serve him. He entices and then kills his victims, often with the very thing he used to entice them. We see this all the time in our world today. People are enticed to use drugs and alcohol, and then many of them die from diseases, accidents, or overdoses related to drugs and alcohol. Others turn to occult practices, only to become the victims of those same practices. Many people are drawn to crave material goods and then pay a high penalty for stealing or embezzling.

Some people believe the devil likes particular people and gives them certain powers. The devil has never liked any human being. Every human being is a potential threat to him. The devil uses people the way a cat plays with a mouse just prior to eating it. The devil has disliked you from your birth, solely because you are a creation of God designed with a specific purpose that is ultimately for your good and God's glory. The devil doesn't want you to bring glory to God or to live a life that points toward God's love. He is your *adversary*, and he will never cease to be your adversary.

The Bible has other names for the devil, all of which describe various aspects of his evil nature:

- Thief (John 10:10)
- Father of lies (John 8:44)
- Beelzebub—ruler of maggots; agent of decay (Matt. 12:27)
- Deceiver (Rev. 12:9)
- Tempter (Matt. 4:3)
- Satan, bringing continual accusation against those who have faith in God (Matt. 12:26).

Not one of these names for the devil is flattering! There is not one ounce of good in him. He is evil to the core. In our study we will use the words *enemy, devil,* and *Satan* interchangeably.

The thief does not come except to steal, and to kill, and to destroy. I have come that they may have life, and that they may have it more abundantly.

—John 10:10

≈ What are the devil's goals in your life, according to this verse? What are Jesus' goals?

≈ When have you seen the powers of the world lead to death or destruction, in your life or the life of someone near you? How did the end result differ from the beginning temptation?

A Satanic Attack

A satanic attack is an experience in which we sense that Satan has launched a major assault against our lives. He is prowling about the edges of our lives at all times, of course, looking for a particular point of entry. His tactic is like that of a pride of lions; to zero in on weakness, divide, and then destroy. When the devil thinks that he has an opening, he attacks. We usually have a general awareness that the devil is not far away, but there are times when we are keenly aware that the devil is making a direct move against us. That is a satanic attack.

Assurance and Warning for the Believer in Christ

If you are a believer in Christ Jesus, you should be assured that the devil cannot destroy your relationship with Christ. He cannot cross the blood barrier that Christ purchased on your behalf when He died on the cross at Calvary. In Christ, we have eternal life (John 3:16; 1 John 5:11–13).

Paul wrote that neither principalities nor powers could separate a person from the love of Christ (Rom. 8:38). *Principalities* and *powers* describe demonic forces. Paul also said that neither height nor depth could separate a person from Christ (Rom. 8:39). *Depth* refers in part to sheol, the place of the dead.

What the devil can do, however, is attack you in the realm of your emotions, your mind, and your body. He moves against you so that you no longer have the energy, the health, the drive, or even much of a desire to serve God. The devil cannot score a definitive victory over you, but he can render you ineffective.

The devil also attacks your reputation and your witness. He always is seeking a means of destroying the testimony of a Christian, again in order to render that Christian ineffective for the gospel's sake. The devil knows he can't take away the eternal life of a believer, but he'll do his best to make the believer *useless* as an advocate for God's kingdom on earth. In other words, the devil may not be able to keep you from heaven, but he will do his best to make certain that you don't take anybody to heaven with you.

For I am persuaded that neither death nor life, nor angels nor principalities nor powers, nor things present nor things to come, nor height nor depth, nor any other created thing, shall be able to separate us from the love of God which is in Christ Jesus our Lord.

—Romans 8:38–39

&. List, in your own words, the things that cannot separate you from the love of God. Is there anything not covered by that list?

&. What does this suggest concerning the attacks of the devil?

Patient and Persistent

Satan is committed to destroying you at any cost. He is patient, willing to wait for the one moment of weakness that he needs to attack you. He is equally persistent; he will not give up seeking your destruction. We are very unwise if we think that we ever have a respite from the devil, or if we think that we have conquered him once and for all in our lives, or even in one particular area of our lives. He continues to prowl, to wait, to watch, to seek a basis to attack us. If he can't influence us directly, he'll attempt to influence others around us in order to divert our attention from Christ or weaken our resolve to walk in purity with Christ.

The only way to ensure that Satan does not gain an opportunity in our lives is to remain close to Christ Jesus and to walk daily in the guidance and strength offered to us by the Holy Spirit. We must keep our resolve to say no to the temptation to sin and to seek God's forgiveness quickly anytime we fail to keep God's commandments.

> If we say that we have no sin, we deceive ourselves, and the truth is not in us. If we confess our sins, He is faithful and just to forgive us our sins and to cleanse us from all unrighteousness.

> —1 John 1:8–9

How does Satan sometimes deceive people into denying sin? When have you seen this in your own life?

What is God's command concerning our sins? What role does God play in this process? What role do you play?

What Satan Can and Cannot Do

As powerful and cunning as Satan may be, he is neither omnipotent nor omniscient. Nor is he omnipresent. In fact, the devil bears none of the absolute or everlasting qualities of God.

The devil was originally created by God as Lucifer, one of the archangels of heaven. As a created being, he had a beginning and he will have a horrible ending: destruction and torment in a lake of fire and brimstone (Rev. 20:10). As a creature, the devil can only be in one place at a time. Many people believe they are doing constant battle with Satan. In all likelihood, they have never had a single battle with Satan himself. The forces they have battled are Satan's demons, the fallen angels who joined Lucifer in rebelling against God. It is primarily through demons that Satan exerts his influence on human beings today.

Demons have the ability to tempt. They have the ability to torment and oppress human beings, including the ability to harass Christians. Paul described demonic activity with Christians as a wrestling match (Eph. 6:11–12). Satan himself does not indwell human beings. To do so would greatly limit his power. Demons, however, have the ability to indwell a non-Christian so that the person begins to act the same way Satan would act if he were present on the scene.

The demons are organized and ruled by Satan. They do what he commands. The Bible tells us that the forces of darkness have a hierarchy. Paul described this to the Ephesians as "principalities ... powers ... rulers of the darkness" (Eph. 6:12). Demonic activity is widespread and constant. In fact, John wrote, "the whole world lies under the sway of the wicked one" (1 John 5:19). The devil, the wicked one, exercises his influence through his demons.

Satan and his demonic forces are powerful and prevalent, but they are not sovereign. Only God is sovereign. Only God possesses ultimate authority over His universe. Satan cannot exceed the limits that God has put upon him, and neither can his demons. God may allow Satan an opportunity to tempt or to exert influence in a person's life, but God determines the extent to which Satan can operate. God retains ultimate control—always.

We see this in the life of Job. Satan asked for access to Job to torment him, and God allowed him to do so (Job 1:6–12; 2:1–6). The first time Satan made this request, the Lord said, "Behold, all that he has is in your power; only do not lay a hand on his person" (Job 1:12). Satan caused the death of Job's sons and daughters, as well as the loss of Job's herds, flocks, and servants, but Job responded by saying, "The Lord gave, and the Lord has taken away; blessed be the name of the Lord" (Job 1:21). He did not blame God for any of his misfortune.

The second time Satan asked permission to tempt Job, the Lord said, "Behold, he is in your hand, but spare his life" (Job 2:6). In both cases, two things are important to note:

First, Satan is subservient to God. He can bring accusations against a person and he can question God, but he cannot touch the person who fears God and shuns evil unless God gives him permission (Job 1:1).

Second, God puts limits on what Satan is allowed to do. Satan cannot overstep the boundaries that God puts upon him.

At the end of Job's story, God says to Job, "Who then is able to stand against Me? Who has preceded Me, that I should pay him? Everything under heaven is Mine" (Job 41:10–11). "Everything" includes, of course, Satan and his demons. Yet part of the deception Satan has played upon the minds of men and women is that he is as powerful as God, that he is equal to God, and that he holds just as much power for evil as God holds for good. That simply is not true. Satan operates *under* God's sovereignty. He is a rebel against a higher authority. God alone is the sovereign King of the universe and He has no equal.

Read Job 1:6–12. What do you learn about Satan from these verses? What do you learn about God?

Why did God draw the devil's attention to Job? What did this suggest about Job's character? About God's power?

Our Response: Healthy Respect, Not Cowering Fear

What should be our response to the devil once we know his nature? I believe we should have a clear understanding of the devil's power, but as Christians we should not cower in fear before him. He is a defeated foe; Christ Jesus our Lord is victor over him. The person who does not have a personal relationship with Christ Jesus is the one who should fear the devil. That person has no shield against the devil and is open prey to the devil's assaults.

If you have not accepted Jesus Christ as your personal Savior and you are not walking closely with Christ today, I encourage you to own up to your sinful nature and recognize that you are living apart from God. Accept Jesus' payment for your sins, ask the Father to forgive you and transform your sin nature, and ask God to fill you with His Holy Spirit so that you might live a life that is pleasing to Him. Unless you are a Christian, you cannot overcome the enemy of your soul. As long as you are a nonbeliever, you are one of the devil's favorite targets. You are destined to be his victim without any recourse as long as you remain in rebellion against God.

> For He says: *"In an acceptable time I have heard you, and in the day of salvation I have helped you."* Behold, now is the accepted time; behold, now is the day of salvation.
>
> —2 Corinthians 6:2

Have you accepted Jesus as your Lord and Savior? If not, what is preventing you from doing so right now?

If you have accepted Christ as your Savior, how are you protected from the devil?

❧ Today and Tomorrow ❧

TODAY: SATAN CANNOT TOUCH A HAIR OF MY HEAD WITHOUT GOD'S PERMISSION.

TOMORROW: I WILL PLACE MY FAITH COMPLETELY IN CHRIST TO PROTECT ME FROM THE DEVIL'S ATTACKS.

❧ Notes and Prayer Requests: ❧

LESSON 3

The Tactics of Our Enemy

———— ❧ **In This Lesson** ❧ ————

LEARNING: WHY DO I WIND UP COMMITTING SIN WHEN I DON'T WANT TO?

GROWING: HOW CAN I PREVENT TEMPTATION BEFORE IT GETS STARTED?

∞

We need to know the nature of the enemy and also his tactics. A knowledge of the devil's methods equips us to discern the devil at work and to know better how to resist him and withstand his assaults. Satan's primary tool is deception. He works in our minds to get us to call good "bad" and bad "good." He is a master of twisting the truth and veiling what is harmful so that it *appears* to be beneficial.

The devil is an expert at appearances, disguises, and false illusions. He is the master counterfeiter. The best counterfeits, of course, are objects that are most like the genuine articles. The devil specializes in "good fakes." He comes at us in a way that is appealing and appears to be very spiritual and totally acceptable. Paul referred to the devil as an "angel of light" who is *masquerading* as one of God's holy angels.

> For Satan himself transforms himself into an angel of light. Therefore it is no great thing if his ministers [demons] also transform themselves into ministers of righteousness, whose end will be according to their works.
>
> —2 Corinthians 11:14–15

Satan's best efforts are when a person under demonic influence *appears* to be doing something that is good or noble, when in fact the person is operating from evil motives and for evil ends. Ultimately, the darkness in an evil person will be revealed and will destroy the person, but often not until many others are deceived and are living according to Satan's purposes.

Satan's best human agents are not the drunks sitting on a downtown street corner or the gang members who terrorize a neighborhood. Everybody knows that these people are the perpetuators of something bad. No, Satan's best agents are the brilliant, well-dressed, "successful" people who claim that they have made their way in life totally on their own intellect and skill, who refuse to acknowledge Jesus Christ, and who are fountains of all sorts of false philosophies. They operate in a wide variety of religions and "isms" around the world—including the religions of secularism and humanism, which worship the idols of human achievement. These expert agents of Satan appear to be well-intentioned people who have the needs and concerns of others at heart. In reality, they are self-centered, godless people who are motivated by a greed for possessions and a lust for personal power.

Satan is often depicted as a bright red creature with a long pointed tail and horns growing out of his head. If Satan really looked like that, nobody would be deceived by him. They would see him coming a mile away! Satan's tactics and "appearance"—which includes the way that his demons work—are much more subtle. Only those who are discerning are able to see him at work.

The more Satan watches our lives and knows about us, the more veiled his tactics become. He rarely attacks a person head-on at his strong points. Rather, he discovers our weaknesses and bores into us over time, chipping away at our lives with persistence and increasing subtlety. It's as if the devil says, "Well, he saw through that and didn't buy my lie, so let me see if I can hide my intent a little and try another tactic that won't be so easily recognized." The more we resist the devil, the more clever and veiled are the devil's deceptions. Over time, this can reach the point where Jesus said that even those who were the strongest, most committed Christians would be in danger of becoming deceived (Matt. 24:24).

🕮 When have you been deceived into thinking that something bad was good, or vice versa?

🕮 Give some examples of good things that the world calls bad, and some bad things that the world calls good.

The Process of Deception

Deception has several identifiable stages.

First, an idea is planted in our imaginations. Everybody has an imagination. It's a part of our thinking that we use for exploring "what if" possibilities and dreams. The imagination is neutral—it can be turned to bad or good. The person who uses his imagination for good can be a positive force for building up God's people and expanding the kingdom of God on earth. Such a person can envision highly innovative ways to spread the gospel and show the love of God to people who are desperately in need of His love. On the other hand, the person who allows his imagination to be used for evil can have an equally dangerous and damaging influence on others.

We must ask ourselves about any new idea, "Where does the implementation of this idea lead?" In other words, will implementation of the idea lead us and others to heaven, or will it lead us or others astray and cause us to be detoured away from heaven? The first thing the devil does to deceive us is to plant an idea in our minds that has an appealing element to it. Usually our first impulse toward Satan's ideas is to reject them. If we do so, we can cut off Satan's efforts before we experience any negative backlash.

Unfortunately, the devil's ideas are always wrapped in some element that appeals to us. He knows what we like and what we want in our fleshly desires, and he wraps up his temptation in something that appeals to us. He does this so that we will at least entertain the idea a while. We may call it a fantasy, daydream, or wish. We know that it's wrong, but we assume there's no harm because we are only *thinking about it.*

The more we dwell on one of Satan's ideas, the more we are trapped by it. We sometimes say that certain things or ideas "capture" our imaginations. In fact, they do! The longer an idea is entertained in the imagination, the more likely we are to act on it.

> For the weapons of our warfare are not carnal but mighty in God for pulling down strongholds, casting down arguments and every high thing that exalts itself against the knowledge of God, bringing every thought into captivity to the obedience of Christ....

> —2 Corinthians 10:4–5

What are the "weapons of our warfare"?

What does it mean to bring every thought into captivity? How is this done?

Second, we begin to identify with the idea that the devil has planted in our imagination. We start to put ourselves into the picture. We wonder how it would feel to own that object or to be with that person or to participate in that activity. The longer we identify with the idea, the more we *desire* to try out the idea. We begin to dwell on the idea, and it occupies more and more of our mental energy. Increasingly, we justify the beneficial and appealing aspects of the idea.

In the 1960s, the counterculture movement spawned the saying, "If it feels good, do it. And if you haven't tried it, don't knock it." We as a nation began to accept the idea that, unless we had personal experience with something, we had no right to criticize it or call it a sin. Satan has taken that philosophy and couched it in even more subtle terms. Now we justify to ourselves that it is acceptable for us to "try out an idea in our minds"—that is, to identify with it in our thoughts. We don't have any real intention of engaging in the actual behavior, primarily because we don't want to be caught in the act by others. We justify to ourselves, however, that it just might be beneficial for us to try out a particular idea in our minds so we can see how we feel about it. We assume that, if we never actually *do* in reality what we are *thinking* in our minds, we remain righteous in God's eyes.

This faulty thinking has been around since Adam and Eve were expelled from the Garden of Eden. Jesus pointed to the danger of *identifying* with sin and responding to it in the mind and heart:

> You have heard that it was said to those of old, "You shall not murder, and whoever murders will be in danger of the judgment." But I say to you that whoever is angry with his brother without a cause shall be in danger of the judgment…. You have heard that it was said to those of old, "You shall not commit adultery." But I say to you that whoever looks at a woman to

lust for her has already committed adultery with her in his
heart.

—Matthew 5:21–22, 27–28

Jesus taught that the way we think is just as real as the way we behave.
Sinning in our minds is just as real as sinning before the whole world.
When we begin to identify with Satan's ideas, we are already in highly
dangerous territory.

Why is it just as sinful to think about adultery as to commit it?

How does this principle apply to other situations?

*Third, we have a growing desire to experience the reality of Satan's sinful
idea, and we begin to plot a way in which we might act it out.* The more
we identify with one of Satan's ideas, the stronger our desire grows to
experience the idea. When that desire reaches a certain degree of inten-
sity, our wills become involved. We begin to make a plan for acting out
the full-blown desire that began as only a prick of our imagination.

Let me give you a couple of examples. A person might start thinking about something he knows he can't afford, perhaps a fancy new convertible sports car that costs three times what he has available to spend on a car. He thinks about how beautiful the car is and then about all the benefits of owning such a car. Before long he is thinking about how good it would feel to drive the car with the top down and about how his friends would be impressed if he owned such a car. He begins to see himself sitting in it. He imagines the car in front of his house, and he fantasizes about driving it to work and parking it in his own special parking place. Soon he is making plans to go for a test drive at a local dealership.

In another example, a woman begins to think about what it might be like to be married to a man she works with. The only problem is that this man is already married. She ignores that fact and starts to think about all the benefits that might be associated with marrying this man. She begins to see herself going places with him and starts to project how envious her friends would be. Before long she is plotting a way to get this man to have lunch with her, in hopes that she might find a way to get him to invite her out to dinner.

There's only a short step between having a strong desire for something and making a plan that puts that desire into action. The Scriptures strongly advise us to check out our plans and the motives behind them.

Fourth, we act out the idea. In acting out an idea, we rarely have an intent of turning the action into a habit. We usually say to ourselves, "I'm just going to try this one time to see what it's like." But if we try something we know to be sin, the part that was appealing to us in the first place is going to be temporarily satisfying, and we are going to continue to desire what we know to be wrong. We try to convince ourselves that we are strong enough to say no to a second temptation, even though we haven't been strong enough to say no to the first temptation.

Once we make a decision to act out sin, we are self-deluded. We think we can control our fleshly tendencies to sin. In reality, our fleshly tendencies are in control of us. When we give in to sin and it becomes a habit in our lives, we become addicted to our sin. It rules us. It dominates our every waking thought. It governs our every action.

Our natural human desires are strong, especially when they are coupled with our human will. Once we engage knowingly in sin, the desire for sin is even stronger and our will to sin is strengthened. We find it increasingly difficult on our own to deny ourselves what we desire. Our willpower diminishes. Only as we trust the Holy Spirit to give us the power to withstand Satan's temptations can we turn away from sin and choose God's plan for good (Rom. 7:15–25).

> For the good that I will to do, I do not do; but the evil I will not to do, that I practice. Now if I do what I will not to do, it is no longer I who do it, but sin that dwells in me.

> —Romans 7:19–20

🔖 Put these verses into your own words. When have you made a similar lament?

✑ Even though Paul says "it is no longer I who commit sin," he is still responsible for his sin. Why?

All Sin Begins with Satan's Ideas

All of us are thinking constantly. Both the Holy Spirit and Satan have access to our minds. We do not think thoughts totally on our own initiative. Our minds, our imaginations, are the soil in which the Holy Spirit plants seed ideas that will bear a harvest of blessing in our lives. In like manner, Satan has been allowed to *attempt* to plant seeds that have no potential other than to become wild weeds of destruction.

We must choose to let the thoughts that are from God remain and take root in us. With great diligence, we must choose to let the thoughts that are from Satan fly right on by. We must refuse to entertain Satan's notions or to engage in fanciful imaginations about evil.

Peter gave us great wisdom about how we can avoid the devil's process of deception: "Be sober, be vigilant" (1 Peter 5:8).

Sober. To be sober means to have a clear mind. We are not to have any fuzzy thinking about what is right and what is wrong. We are to know with certainty the commandments of God and the teachings of Jesus so that we will know instantly if an idea is from Satan or from the Holy

Spirit. It is our responsibility to maintain a sober mind. No one else can read and study God's Word for us. We must do it ourselves. We must set our minds to learn what is right and what is wrong from God's perspective.

To be sober also implies a seriousness about life. We are not to joke about the devil or take him lightly. We are to recognize that we have an enemy who wants only one thing: to wipe us out. If he can't wipe us out, he'll settle for the next best thing: to render us ineffective and useless. We must take our enemy as seriously as he takes us.

Vigilant. To be vigilant means to be watchful and alert, to be quick to say no to the devil. How do we stay vigilant? We ask the Holy Spirit to help us stay vigilant! The devil has never pulled the wool over the eyes of the Holy Spirit. The devil has never deceived the Holy Spirit, whom Jesus described as being the Spirit of truth. Our vigilance is directly related to our reliance upon the Holy Spirit to guide us in our daily decisions and choices. If we ask the Holy Spirit with a sincere heart to reveal to us the lies of the devil and to help us discern evil spirits at work, we can be assured that He will do so.

God has never asked us to overcome the enemy on our own strength. He gives us the Holy Spirit to help us overcome the enemy. We, however, must choose to receive the Holy Spirit's help. Being sober and being vigilant mean being serious about following God in every area of our lives, twenty-four hours a day, every day.

> And do not be conformed to this world, but be transformed by the renewing of your mind, that you may prove what is that good and acceptable and perfect will of God.
>
> —Romans 12:2

❧ What does it mean to be conformed to this world? How does this happen?

❧ What does it mean to renew your mind? How is this done?

❧ Why is a renewed mind essential if we are to understand the will of God?

❧ Today and Tomorrow ❧

TODAY: THE DEVIL TRIES TO TURN MY MIND TO EVIL, BUT THE HOLY SPIRIT WILL TURN IT TO GOOD.

TOMORROW: I WILL ASK THE LORD TO HELP ME TRANSFORM MY THINKING THIS WEEK.

LESSON 4

A Posture of Active Resistance

❧ In This Lesson ☙

LEARNING: IF THE DEVIL IS SO POWERFUL, HOW CAN I HOPE TO DEFEAT
HIM?

GROWING: WHAT IS MY ROLE IN THIS STRUGGLE, AND WHAT IS GOD'S
ROLE?

Throughout history we have many examples of people who resisted evil in ways that were not militant, vengeful, or violent. In fact, most of the Christian martyrs through the ages took a stand against evil, refusing to deny the Lord Jesus, to turn their back on their faith, or to expose their fellow Christians to harm. Their resistance made a difference, and in the end Christ was proved victor. Christ's kingdom on earth expands, while man-made kingdoms fade into history.

Resistance is the biblical approach to confronting and overcoming the devil. Peter wrote, "Resist him, steadfast in the faith" (1 Peter 5:9). James echoed this teaching: "Submit to God. Resist the devil and he will flee from you. Draw near to God and He will draw near to you" (James 4:7–8). Both Peter and James make clear that we are to actively resist evil.

Active Resistance

On the surface resistance may appear to be passive, but it is anything but passive in actual practice. It is an active stance that is intentional and powerful. Think about what you would do if you saw a large person running directly toward you at a rapid pace. Imagine that there is a sheer wall to your right and a sharp drop-off to your left. There's no way you can turn and outrun this adversary. What do you do? You very likely brace yourself for the hit. You plant your feet squarely and lean forward, probably with one shoulder and leg a little ahead of your other leg and shoulder. You grit your teeth, tense your muscles, and prepare for the blow, fully expecting that your adversary will bounce off you rather than knock you down. You are in a position of resistance.

Resistance is rowing against the tide of the culture and refusing to adopt evil practices, even though the people around us may be adopting them. Resistance is doing the right thing, solely because it is the right thing to do. Resistance is saying no to offers of drugs and other harmful substances. Resistance is first and foremost a firm decision to engage in the struggle against evil, rather than backing off or retreating from the devil's attack.

> Therefore submit to God. Resist the devil and he will flee from you.
>
> —James 4:7

What does it mean to submit to God? To resist the devil? Give specific examples of each.

🐟 When have you deliberately chosen to resist evil? What were the circumstances? What were the results?

Resistance and Patience

Resistance takes strength and courage. It also takes patience.

> Be patient, brethren, until the coming of the Lord. See how the farmer waits for the precious fruit of the earth, waiting patiently for it until it receives the early and latter rain. You also be patient. Establish your hearts.
>
> —James 5:7–8

We are to be patient with ourselves, and we are to be patient with our fellow believers. We must look with hope to the future that the Lord has for each one of us. The good work that He is doing in us, He is also doing in others around us, perhaps in different ways and at a different pace. If we become impatient with our spiritual growth or that of others, it is easy to become angry, frustrated, and unloving. Such attitudes give an opportunity for Satan to work. They are not attitudes of resistance. Resistance is patient.

Love suffers long and is kind; love does not envy; love does not parade itself, is not puffed up.

—1 Corinthians 13:4

✎ What does it mean to "parade" oneself? To be puffed up? How is love different from these?

✎ How can envy make a person impatient with others? How does "suffering long" work to defeat envy?

How to Resist

Peter and James point to two key words that are at the heart of our ability to resist the devil: *submission* to God and *faith*.

Submission. Submission to God is saying, "I can't, but You can." In our resistance against the devil, we might say, "I can't defeat the devil on my own, but with You, I can." Certainly this is the position that the apostle Paul took when he said, "I can do all things through Christ who strengthens me" (Phil. 4:13).

James described submission as developing a closer relationship to God: "Draw near to God and He will draw near to you" (James 4:8). The number one way to know God and to know how He wants us to overcome evil is to spend time with Him. It's virtually impossible to have a close relationship with someone if you have no communication! We draw near to God in prayer and in time spent reading His Word. We draw near to God when we set aside time solely to listen to Him and to wait upon Him for direction and guidance. We draw near to God when we periodically shut ourselves away with Him, closing off all other influences that might distract us from knowing Him better.

The closer we draw to God, the better we know Him. And the better we know Him, the more we see His awesome power, experience His vast love, learn from His wisdom, and grow in our faith. We come to an even greater realization and conclusion: "Yes, God *can* defeat the devil on my behalf."

Those who submit their lives to God are humble. Humility and submission cannot be separated. The truly humble recognize that they are totally dependent upon God and that only God is God. The person who believes the truth about God with all of his heart receives an abundant portion of God's grace (James 4:6).

Humble yourselves in the sight of the Lord, and He will lift you up.

—James 4:10

🙉 What does it mean to humble yourself in the sight of the Lord? How is this done?

🙉 When have you deliberately humbled yourself in the past? What were the circumstances? What were the results?

Faith. Faith is saying to God, "I believe that You will." In our battle to overcome the enemy, our faith might be stated this way: "I believe that You will defeat the enemy and cause him to flee from me as I resist him and put my trust in You." Again and again, David made this declaration of faith to the Lord: "O my God, I trust in You" (Pss. 25:2; 31:6; 55:23; 56:3; 143:8).

Each of us has been given a measure of faith from our birth (Rom. 12:3), but this does not mean that we automatically have an active, vibrant, or mature faith. Our faith can lie dormant in us, for the most part unused. It also can remain a weak or immature faith. Jesus referred to "great faith" and "little faith" (Matt. 6:30; 8:10, 26). The disciples asked specifically that Jesus increase their faith (Luke 17:5). The implication is clearly that our faith is capable of growth.

Our faith becomes alive and active when we recognize who we are in Christ. "Christ in me" is one of the most powerful statements of faith a person can make, for Christ has far greater power than any force of the devil (1 John 4:4). We grow in faith by using our faith, by trusting God in situation after situation, circumstance after circumstance, relationship after relationship. We develop a personal history in which we have been faithful in our obedience to God and He has been faithful in His loving care of us.

The Bible speaks frequently about walking in faith or standing in faith. *Faith is to be applied.* It is to be exercised and developed. When we stand in faith, we are saying, "I am fully persuaded that God is God, and I cannot be moved from that position." When we walk in faith, we are saying, "I have every confidence that God is with me wherever I am, and that He will remain with me forever. I am fully convinced that He is working all things together for my eternal and highest good" (Rom. 8:28).

Remaining steadfast in our faith is an act of our will. We must *choose* to remain steadfast in faith—staying grounded, keeping our resolve, refusing to give in to doubt or fear. The Holy Spirit will help us in this if we ask for His help. He is the One who gives us the power to endure the assault of the enemy against us, even to the last moment of our lives.

But thanks be to God, who gives us the victory through our Lord Jesus Christ. Therefore, my beloved brethren, be steadfast, immovable, always abounding in the work of the Lord, knowing that your labor is not in vain in the Lord.

—1 Corinthians 15:57–58

∽ What does it mean to be steadfast? Immovable? Give real-life examples of each.

∽ Why is it important to understand that "your labor is not in vain in the Lord"? What does this phrase mean?

Faith, Submission, and Resistance Are Connected

In the battle against our adversary, our faith in Christ Jesus, our submission to God, and our resistance against the enemy are closely connected. You can resist the devil only if your faith is strong. It is impossible for you to resist the devil for very long if you do not believe that Christ Jesus in you can and will defeat the devil.

Furthermore, you can be firm in your faith only if you are completely submissive to God. That means that you submit all areas of your life. When you do not submit an area to God, you are saying, "I can handle this. I don't need Your help." That's precisely the place where the devil will attack you!

The good news is that God has given each of us a measure of faith to develop. We are capable of submitting, and therefore we are capable of resisting the devil. When we do, he must flee.

> I beseech you therefore, brethren, by the mercies of God, that you present your bodies a living sacrifice, holy, acceptable to God, which is your reasonable service.

> —Romans 12:1

☙ What does it mean to present your body as a living sacrifice? How is this done? Why is it "your reasonable service"?

☙ What part does this "self sacrifice" play in resisting the devil? In what ways must we stand firm with our bodies before we can resist the devil?

❧ Today and Tomorrow ❧

TODAY: THE LORD HAS PROMISED ME THAT THE DEVIL WILL FLEE IF I RESIST HIM.

TOMORROW: I WILL ASK THE LORD EACH DAY TO SHOW ME HOW TO AC-TIVELY RESIST THE ENEMY.

❧ Notes and Prayer Requests: ❧

LESSON 5

Developing a Discerning Spirit

───────── ℚ **In This Lesson** ℛ ─────────

LEARNING: WHAT DOES IT MEAN TO HAVE A DISCERNING SPIRIT?

GROWING: HOW CAN I ATTAIN DISCERNMENT?

Many of God's people are in trouble today because they do not have a discerning spirit. They walk right into Satan's traps and never even know what happened to them. Then they say, "I can't imagine what went wrong." A person with a discerning spirit will be able to point out Satan's trap and how they fell into it.

Each of us needs to develop a discerning spirit and to teach our children how to have a discerning spirit. A discerning spirit is rooted in a knowledge of right and wrong. The time to begin teaching discernment, the difference between right and wrong, is not when the children have reached adulthood. We teach it to them from their early youth.

Moses told the Israelites that they must thoroughly train their children in God's commandments:

> And these words which I command you today shall be in your heart. You shall teach them diligently to your children, and shall talk of them when you sit in your house, when you walk by the way, when you lie down, and when you rise up. You shall

bind them as a sign on your hand, and they shall be as frontlets between your eyes. You shall write them on the doorposts of your house and on your gates.

—Deuteronomy 6:6–9

We must know right from wrong, both in theory and in practice. We must know how to apply God's truth to our lives and how to live in obedience to His commandments. That's why Moses said that we are to teach our children God's commandments throughout the day, not just in a half-hour Sunday school lesson. We are to say plainly to them, "This is right behavior; this is wrong behavior. This is God's commandment. This is the consequence of breaking God's commandment." An education in right and wrong must occur twenty-four hours a day, every day of the year.

A child who is thoroughly trained in God's commandments, who has been taught right from wrong, has very little trouble discerning Satan at work. He quickly picks up signals that tell him when things are not right; his conscience is sensitive. The child who has not been taught right from wrong, on the other hand, becomes a slow-moving target for the enemy. A child who is allowed to do whatever he wants, or who has been taught that everything is relative and there are no absolutes, will be an easy prey for Satan.

There have been times when I've entered a room full of people and immediately sensed in my spirit that something was not right. It's as if an inner alarm had gone off. At times, the room was even occupied by a group of Christians, but my inner spiritual radar told me that something was amiss, something wasn't right before God. In every case, I've discovered that this inner discernment was correct.

Each Christian must be developing and exercising this kind of spiritual discernment. God does not want His people to live in darkness or to be without an ability to detect evil at work. He has made every provision necessary for us to acquire and grow in our ability to discern our enemy.

God's provision for us is twofold: His Word and His Spirit. The Bible is our sourcebook for right and wrong. God's Spirit is our teacher in helping us to choose good in our daily walk with Christ.

> For everyone who partakes only of milk is unskilled in the word of righteousness, for he is a babe. But solid food belongs to those who are of full age, that is, those who by reason of use have their senses exercised to discern both good and evil.

> —Hebrews 5:13–14

✍ What "milk" and "solid food" are meant in these verses? What distinguishes "milk" from "solid food"?

✍ What is needed, according to these verses, to distinguish between good and evil?

The Critical Importance of Knowing God's Principles

You will grow in your knowledge of right and wrong only by remaining steadfastly in God's Word. If your parents did not teach you right from wrong at an early age, it is imperative that you retrain your mind. You can do this by reading God's Word on a consistent, daily basis.

Believe what you read; accept God's Word at face value. God means what He says and says what He means. Apply what you read. Put God's Word to use by doing what it says.

God's Word will renew your mind as you read it, giving you increasing insight into what God considers to be righteous and unrighteous behavior and attitudes. As you read God's Word on a daily basis, your very desires will begin to change. You will no longer feel drawn to or comfortable in harmful settings. You will develop a deep intuitive understanding that you simply do not belong in certain relationships.

Even if you had a wonderful Christ-centered childhood, you will benefit greatly by staying in God's Word on a daily basis. What you have learned in the past is reinforced in your mind and heart. So much in our culture is upside-down: right is called wrong and wrong is called right. Blame is placed everywhere except where it belongs: on the exercise of free will that God gave each of us. A steady and consistent reading of God's commandments helps to keep us from falling victim to false teachings and human philosophies.

> Guard what was committed to your trust, avoiding the profane and idle babblings and contradictions of what is falsely called knowledge—by professing it some have strayed concerning the faith.

> —1 Timothy 6:20–21

✒ What is Paul referring to that has been "committed to your trust"? What must be done for you to guard it?

✒ What "profane and idle babblings and contradictions" does the world teach today? List some examples below.

✒ How does God's Word refute such teachings of the world?

The Simplicity of the Truth

Don't try to complicate or read your own meanings into God's Word. God has not made His Word too difficult for you to comprehend. You may benefit from a translation of the Scriptures that presents God's truth in more modern English so that you can better understand the language of the Bible. But the *truths* of the Bible are actually quite plain. We are the ones who make the Bible complicated in our attempts to justify our own desire to sin or to explain away the passages that we find difficult to obey.

Paul warned the Corinthians that "as the serpent deceived Eve by his craftiness, so your minds may be corrupted from the simplicity that is in Christ" (2 Corinthians 11:3). Satan came to Eve in the Garden of Eden and asked, "Has God indeed said...?" He planted a doubt in her mind. He implied that God might not actually have commanded Adam not to eat of the forbidden fruit, or perhaps that they had misinterpreted God's words. Eve began to read into God's commandment more than God had said. She replied, "God has said, 'You shall not eat it, nor shall you touch it, lest you die'" (Gen. 3:3). Those were not God's exact words, however. He had told Adam, "of the tree of the knowledge of good and evil you shall not eat, for in the day that you eat of it you shall surely die" (Gen. 2:17). Eve added something to God's Word.

Next, Satan tried to get Eve to believe that it would be good for her to eat the fruit of the tree because it would make her more like God. If she was more like God, she wouldn't die, because God will never die. Satan complicated the message. He introduced confusion and questioning. If Eve had stayed obedient to God's plain and simple commandment, she would have been fine. The commandment was straightforward and easy to understand. The same is true for virtually all of Gods' commandments.

If you do not understand parts of God's Word, ask God to reveal what you need to know to live in a way that is pleasing to Him. The fact is, you may not need to have a full understanding of the depth of every verse in the Bible. Some of the information in the Bible is likely to be understood fully only after we are with the Lord in heaven. But we can be assured that God will reveal everything that we need to live godly lives each day. We can trust the Holy Spirit to teach us and to remind us of the truth we need as we face specific situations and decisions.

> If any of you lacks wisdom, let him ask of God, who gives to all liberally and without reproach, and it will be given to him.
>
> —James 1:5

Make a list below of any area of life where you need wisdom. Then pray through the list asking God for wisdom in each item. Refer back to this list in the future as God reveals His wisdom to you.

Getting Rid of the Clutter

Much of what we take into our minds is of no eternal use. Is has virtually no benefit in helping us live our daily lives. It serves as clutter and it results in confusion. We need to turn to God's Word on a daily basis, and we need to turn *away* from the messages of the world.

We must refuse to listen to false teachers, those who may appear to be Christians but who do not help others to walk in close relationship with God. We must also refuse to listen to teachers of falsehood, who present messages to us that are impure, violent, rooted in greed, or portray humans as the center of the universe.

> Be diligent to present yourself approved to God, a worker who does not need to be ashamed, rightly dividing the word of truth.

> —2 Timothy 2:15

What does it mean to be "rightly dividing the word of truth"? How is this done?

How does a Christian present himself "approved to God"? Are there areas in your own life of which you might one day be ashamed?

Staying Sensitive to Your Surroundings

Many Christians have suffered because they had no spiritual sensitivity to what was happening around them. We must ask the Holy Spirit to help us remain alert and aware of the opportunities and temptations that come our way.

Throughout the Scriptures we find the admonition to watch. We are to watch so that we can guard against enemy attack. We are also to watch for what the Lord brings our way; we are to remain sensitive always to the blessings and opportunities the Lord sends us. We must watch for ways in which God wants to use us to bring blessings to others.

In ancient times, watchmen were assigned to stand on the walls of fortified cities. They worked in shifts that provided round-the-clock coverage. Their responsibility was twofold: watch for the enemy and watch for the king. Our role as discerning Christians today is the same: we are to watch for the Lord's appearance in our midst as much as we must be alert to the attacks of our enemy.

This means that we must be continually alert for ways to share the gospel. We must be aware of what God wants to do in our lives as we serve as ambassadors for Christ. We must be on constant alert for opportunities to do good and to give encouragement to our fellow Christians. Ask the Lord to help you "watch." He will quickly answer your prayer.

But the end of all things is at hand; therefore be serious and watchful in your prayers.

—1 Peter 4:7

☙ What does it mean to be serious in your prayers? To be watchful?

☙ Why are these things important in prayer?

Remain in Submission to God

The flip side of submission is reliance. When you are submitted to someone, you are at the same time reliant on that person. For example, when you yield your personal defense to another person, you become reliant on that person to protect you. When you submit your ability to provide for yourself, you become reliant on another person for your daily needs. When you submit to the decision-making authority of another person, you become reliant on that person to exercise wisdom on your behalf.

This is a very important concept related to spiritual discernment. With our finite mental ability, we simply cannot discern clearly all of the tactics of the devil. The devil is not omnipotent, but he is more powerful than any human being. The devil is not omniscient, but he knows more than any human being. The devil is not omnipresent, but he's been around a lot longer than any human being. The result is that the devil has cunning tricks that are beyond our abilities to understand.

In order to exercise sound spiritual discernment, you must submit to God's authority and become reliant on His discerning power to work in you. Your submission to God includes submission to the authority of His Word. God expects you to do what He tells you. As you obey His commandments, He takes on the responsibility for all of the consequences related to your obedience. When you trust God's Word to be true, it is then up to God to be faithful to His Word and to perform what He has said He would do on your behalf.

Your submission to God also includes submission to the authority of the Holy Spirit over your life. As a Christian, you are not abandoned to survive on your own in an evil world. But neither are you given free reign to do whatever you want to do. You are in a line of authority under God the Father, and the Holy Spirit is your immediate supervisor. Submission to and reliance on the Holy Spirit must be ongoing in your life; it is a daily submission, not a one-time event.

Our prayer must be this:

> Holy Spirit, I submit myself to You. I want to do only what You want me to do. I want to shun evil and pursue good. I am trusting You to reveal to me any sin in my life, any error that I am about to make. I want to be totally reliant on You to show me which choice to make, which path to pursue, which opportunity to seize, which relationship to forge, which call to answer.

I am also totally reliant on You to reveal to me the presence of evil or attack of the devil on my life and to show me how I might resist the devil and overcome him. Please help me.

Discernment Develops as We Stay Focused on God

Our ability to discern develops as we:

❧ stay in the Word on a daily basis.

❧ stay sensitive to what is happening around us and to those who may be in need.

❧ stay submitted to God's commandments and to the daily direction of the Holy Spirit.

Our focus must be tightly on God and His plans, purposes, and principles. When we are walking closely with the Holy Spirit, discernment comes naturally and quickly. Discernment is critical if we are to sidestep the traps the devil has set for us. In fact, discernment is the key to avoiding many of life's troubles and trials.

You are all sons of light and sons of the day. We are not of the night nor of darkness. Therefore let us not sleep, as others do, but let us watch and be sober.

—1 Thessalonians 5:5–6

❧ What does it mean to be "sons of light"? "Sons of the day"?

What responsibilities do these roles of sonship bring with them?

What does it mean to sleep? To be sober?

Today and Tomorrow

TODAY: THE HOLY SPIRIT WANTS TO GIVE ME MORE WISDOM AND DISCERNMENT.

TOMORROW: I WILL ASK THE LORD EACH DAY THIS WEEK TO GIVE ME WISDOM AND DISCERNMENT.

LESSON 6

Engaging in Warfare

┌─────────────── ❧ **In This Lesson** ❧ ───────────────┐

LEARNING: IS THERE REALLY A SPIRITUAL WAR GOING ON TODAY?

GROWING: HOW CAN I FIGHT SOMEONE THAT I CAN'T EVEN SEE?

└──────────────────────── ❧ ────────────────────────┘

No member of the military engages in warfare on his own initiative. Specific orders must come from those who have the authority to wage war. Even the President of the United States, the commander in chief of the military, cannot declare war without an act of Congress. In the body of Christ, we are under the authority of our spiritual commander in chief, Jesus Christ our Lord. He is the One who authorizes us to engage in warfare against the devil.

This is an important concept to understand. We *do* have the authority to fight the devil. That authority has been given to each of us by Jesus. At the same time, if Jesus had not given us that authority, we would have no basis on which to fight our enemy and no chance of overcoming him. Our battle orders against Satan come from Jesus and from Him alone. He is our commander in the battle. He is the One who fights on our behalf and wins the victory.

Matthew 12 records Jesus' response to the Pharisees when they accused Him of casting out demons by the power of Beelzebub, the ruler of the demons. Jesus' statement conveys an important message to us today as we battle our adversary:

Every kingdom divided against itself is brought to desolation, and every city or house divided against itself will not stand. If Satan casts out Satan, he is divided against himself. How then will his kingdom stand? And if I cast out demons by Beelzebub, by whom do your sons cast them out? Therefore they shall be your judges. But if I cast out demons by the Spirit of God, surely the kingdom of God has come upon you. Or how can one enter a strong man's house and plunder his goods, unless he first binds the strong man? And then he will plunder his house. He who is not with Me is against Me, and he who does not gather with Me scatters abroad.

—Matthew 12:25–30

Jesus told the Pharisees:

- If Satan casts out Satan, he is divided against himself.

- Every kingdom divided against itself will not stand.

- If a person is not with Me in battling demonic power, He is against Me.

If we are not one hundred percent with Jesus in battling our adversary, then we are actually working against Him and our efforts will fail—if we are relying on any other source of power apart from that of the Holy Spirit of God. We cannot defeat the devil with our intellect, with our clever reasoning, or even with our hatred of evil. We can defeat the devil only by relying completely on Jesus Christ to work in us and on our behalf. There is no successful warfare against the devil apart from Him. He authorizes our war against the devil, even as He empowers us to win it and gives us the courage to engage in it.

He who is not with Me is against Me, and he who does not gather with Me scatters abroad.

—Matthew 12:30

❧ What is required of you to be with Jesus rather than against Him?

❧ What does it mean to "gather with" Him? How is this done, in practical terms? How well do you do this?

Assurance of Victory

When we engage in warfare at Christ's command and under His authority, we are assured of victory. When it feels as if we're losing the battle, there are two key points to keep in mind:

1. *The loss of a battle is not the loss of the war.* In some cases, you may have lost a round in your fight against the devil. You may experience a setback. When Jesus sent out His disciples to preach the gospel and

heal the sick, He said that if the people in a city did not receive them, they were to wipe the dust of that place from their feet, give a warning to the people, and move on. Jesus anticipated that His disciples would not be successful one hundred percent of the time.

Nevertheless, Jesus expected His disciples to continue to move forward, doing the maximum amount of good and preaching and praying with the greatest amount of effectiveness. He expects the same of us. He calls us to be faithful, not successful. We are to do what He calls us to do; the consequences and results are His responsibility.

2. The final victory will be revealed fully in eternity. You do not know the full impact that you have on the lives of others. Some of what you accomplish for Christ on earth will be revealed to you only in eternity. And when it comes to eternity, the devil has absolutely no hold on you once you have accepted Christ as your Savior and Lord. Nothing the devil can do to you will change your eternal destiny.

When Jesus sent out seventy of His disciples, two by two, He gave them specific instructions to preach the gospel and heal the sick, which included anything that might keep a person from being whole. The disciples returned to Jesus with great joy, saying, "Lord, even the demons are subject to us in Your name" (Luke 10:17). Jesus responded:

> I saw Satan fall like lightning from heaven. Behold, I give you the authority to trample on serpents and scorpions, and over all the power of the enemy, and nothing shall by any means hurt you.
>
> —Luke 10:18–19

Throughout the Scriptures, *serpents* and *scorpions* are other terms for demons. Jesus told His disciples then, and He tells us today, that His followers have authority over the devil, and the devil can do nothing to cause eternal harm to those who call on the authority of Christ. We may get scared and feel pain from time to time, but we will not experience any eternal damage.

> Watch, stand fast in the faith, be brave, be strong. Let all that you do be done with love.
>
> —1 Corinthians 16:13–14

Why does Paul command us to be brave and strong? What role does your will play in being strong and courageous?

Why is courage important when facing the devil? What is the source of that courage?

What Does Jesus Authorize Us to Do?

The question then naturally arises: What does Jesus authorize us to do in battling our adversary?

First, Jesus expects us to enter Satan's domain with boldness, but only after we have "bound the strong man," which is the demonic entity that has a hold on a person. When confronting the Pharisees, Jesus referred to the power it takes to enter a strong man's house (Matt. 12:29). Jesus laid claim to all the power necessary to walk into the devil's domain, pick up those whom the devil had maimed or oppressed, and bring them out of the devil's prison so that they might be delivered and made whole. He could do this because He was able first to bind the devil.

If we are to enter the devil's domain, we must first bind the strong man who holds power over a person—even if that person is you. We do this by keeping God's commandments, speaking God's words, and doing God's works. Keep in mind that there are all types of bondage. Some people are bound today by habits that they can't seem to break. Others are bound in relationships with people who are committed to evil. The Word of God and the love of God's people are sufficient for breaking *all* types of bondage. There isn't a form of bondage that cannot be broken by the Lord, if we will say and do what the Lord requires of us.

Jesus said, "Whatever you bind on earth will be bound in heaven, and whatever you loose on earth will be loosed in heaven" (Matt. 18:18). We bind the forces of evil by praying against them and resisting them. As we discussed in a previous lesson, we resist by submitting ourselves completely to God and standing firm in our faith. If we are walking in close friendship with Christ Jesus, we render the forces of evil ineffective. We have them bottled up, tied up, locked up. They have no toehold against us. They are "bound" in their efforts to tempt us or harm our eternal spirits.

We loose the force of God's saving love and grace on the earth by giving our witness for Christ Jesus, both in word and in deed, by loving others, and by forgiving those who have sinned against us.

But I say to you who hear: Love your enemies, do good to those who hate you, bless those who curse you, and pray for those who spitefully use you.

—Luke 6:27–28

🖎 Make a list below (which is for your use only—don't share it) of people who have hurt you in some way. Pray for at least one person on the list each day this coming week.

Second, we are to limit the access that Satan has to our lives. Jesus spoke of entering a strong man's house. This concept of entering is not limited to our moving into the devil's domain. The broader principle that Jesus taught includes the truth that we must not allow the devil entrance into our own house where he might cause us harm.

As a believer in Christ, you have authority over what you will allow to enter your life. You have the power to control your thoughts. You have the power to determine what you will put into your body and how you will relate to people. You have the power to develop your own faith and to instill good spiritual disciplines into your life. You have the power to change your habits, perspectives, and attitudes.

Keep your heart with all diligence, for out of it spring the issues of life.

—Proverbs 4:23

≈ What does it mean to "keep your heart"? How is this done? Why is it so important?

≈ How does Satan try to pollute your heart and mind? What can you do to prevent it?

Third, Jesus is present in the binding process of our adversary. Indeed, He is the One who does the binding. Jesus said to Peter and His disciples:

On this rock I will build My church, and the gates of Hades shall not prevail against it. And I will give you the keys of the kingdom of heaven, and whatever you bind on earth will be bound in heaven, and whatever you loose on earth will be loosed in heaven.

—Matthew 16:18–19

The rock to which Jesus referred was Peter's great statement of faith about Jesus: "You are the Christ, the Son of the living God" (Matt. 16:16). That is the central truth of our faith. The "gates of Hades" cannot defeat the church which teaches that Jesus is the Son of the living God. In the time of Jesus the gates of a city were the place of government and authority. All key decisions were made by those who sat in the city gates. Jesus was saying that the power of the devil, the demonic authorities of hell itself, cannot win against a Christ-focused church. The church, of course, is composed of all who have accepted Jesus as their Savior and are following Him as their Lord. We are a part of the greater church and this message of Christ is for us—hell cannot win against us.

Jesus said that He gives the "keys of the kingdom of heaven" to those who are in His church. When you hold the keys to a place, you determine who goes into it. You control the access. Again, the devil cannot enter an area of your life unless you give him access to that area.

Finally, Jesus assures us that what we do to bind the devil's power on earth is accomplished and sealed definitely and eternally in heaven. And anything that Jesus does has eternal consequences!

✎ Put Matthew 16:18–19 into your own words. What does it mean to bind and to loose something on earth?

What did Jesus mean when He gave His disciples the keys to the kingdom of heaven? How does this apply to you as a follower of Christ?

You Aren't Expected to Fight a War by Yourself

Jesus taught that there is great power in agreement. An individual is not to engage in spiritual warfare on his own. None of us is called to be an army of one. We are to live and work and give witness and engage in warfare against our enemy as the *body* of Christ. Jesus said:

> If two of you agree on earth concerning anything that they ask, it will be done for them by My Father in heaven. For where two or three are gathered together in My name, I am there in the midst of them.
>
> —Matthew 18:19–20

Some spiritual battles may be intensely personal. Nevertheless, I encourage you to find at least one other person who can be a prayer partner with you as you resist the devil and pray for God's will to be accomplished in your life. You are likely to find that you are able to engage in your battle with greater courage and bring the battle to a successful end much more quickly if you ask for the prayers of others. God does not intend for us to live our spiritual lives in isolation.

Confess your trespasses to one another, and pray for one another, that you may be healed. The effective, fervent prayer of a righteous man avails much.

—James 5:16

What does James mean by "effective, fervent prayer"?

Spend time in your study group sharing prayer requests. Write them below, then refer back to this list in prayer this week at least once a day.

Our Spiritual Armor

Paul described our warfare against the devil:

> Be strong in the Lord and in the power of His might. Put on the whole armor of God, that you may be able to stand against the wiles of the devil. For we do not wrestle against flesh and blood, but against principalities, against powers, against the rulers of the darkness of this age, against spiritual hosts of wickedness in the heavenly places. Therefore take up the whole armor of God, that you may be able to withstand in the evil day, and having done all, to stand. Stand therefore, having girded your waist with truth, having put on the breastplate of righteousness, and having shod your feet with the preparation of the gospel of peace; above all, taking the shield of faith with which you will be able to quench all the fiery darts of the wicked one. And take the helmet of salvation, and the sword of the Spirit, which is the word of God; praying always with all prayer and supplication in the Spirit, being watchful to this end with all perseverance and supplication for all the saints.
>
> —Ephesians 6:10–18

I want you to notice four key things about this passage of Scripture:

First, our warfare is spiritual. We must never become confused and think that our warfare is against a particular person or group. The evil that exists in our world today has its origins in the spiritual realm, and we are to go directly to the source of the evil and do our fighting there.

Second, the armor that we put on is Christ. Every piece of armor that Paul described is directly related to Jesus. We are to put on the truth of Jesus, the righteousness of Jesus, the gospel of peace embodied in

Jesus, faith in Jesus as God's Son, and the salvation that Jesus purchased for us. We are to pick up the Word of God—upon which Jesus based all His words—as if it is our sword. Every facet of our defense against our adversary is acquired when we "put on Christ Jesus."

> But put on the Lord Jesus Christ, and make no provision for the flesh, to fulfill its lusts.
>
> —Romans 13:14

What does it mean to "put on Christ"? How is this done?

What does it mean to "make provision for the flesh"? How can you avoid this, in practical terms?

We put on Christ with our faith. What we believe about Christ we must actively receive into our lives. We then must speak and act as if we have what we believe we have! We say to the Lord:

> "I believe that Jesus is God's only begotten Son and that He died on the cross for me and for the forgiveness of my sins. I believe that You will preserve and protect my spirit so that I might have eternal life with You in heaven."

> "I believe that You are the way, the truth, and the life and that, if I follow the leading of Your Holy Spirit, You will never lead me astray. I trust You to show me what to do in the situation that I am facing right now."

> "I believe that Your righteousness is imparted to me through the Holy Spirit and that, as I obey Your commandments, You will manifest Your character traits in me."

> "I believe that the path which You have for me is for my good and that I will experience Your peace as I walk in it."

Third, our posture in warfare is primarily one of resistance. Only one piece of the armor has an offensive use. Every other aspect is for our defense, so we might "withstand in the evil day," "quench the fiery darts of the wicked one," and be able to "stand."

Fourth, once we have put on Christ, we are to pray. We stand in the presence of God Himself. We come to Him in prayer. Before we take any other action, we are to pray. Prayer is the first thing that we must do anytime we are under attack by the enemy. We are to pray with perseverance—with enduring power—until God's supernatural power is released in us. We are to be watchful in our prayers, alert and diligent. By putting on Christ, standing, and praying, we will be "strong in the

71

Lord and in the power of His might" (Eph. 6:10). When we are strong in Christ, we cannot be defeated!

> Stand therefore, having girded your waist with truth, having put on the breastplate of righteousness, and having shod your feet with the preparation of the gospel of peace; above all, taking the shield of faith with which you will be able to quench all the fiery darts of the wicked one. And take the helmet of salvation, and the sword of the Spirit, which is the word of God;
>
> —Ephesians 6:14–17

What does each piece of armor do? How is each used? What is the spiritual equivalent of each?

Belt:

Breastplate:

Shoes:

Shield:

Helmet:

Sword:

❧ Today and Tomorrow ❧

TODAY: THE DEVIL IS ACTIVELY FIGHTING AGAINST ME, BUT GOD PROVIDES ME WITH ARMOR AND POWER.

TOMORROW: I WILL ASK THE LORD TO SHOW ME HOW TO PUT ON EACH PIECE OF SPIRITUAL ARMOR.

Three Things the Enemy Hates to Hear

❧ In This Lesson ☙

LEARNING: WHAT POWERS DO I HAVE TO FIGHT AGAINST SATAN?

GROWING: HOW DO I USE MY SPIRITUAL WEAPONS?

Have you ever avoided someone solely because you didn't like what that person had to say? Perhaps he used profane or filthy language that offended you. Or perhaps he always made negative comments. Some non-Christians dislike being around Christians because they don't like hearing about Jesus, God's love, the work of the church, or the ministry of the Holy Spirit. Each of us is uncomfortable around certain people because of what they talk about, and the devil is uncomfortable around Christians who talk about things that he hates. Three things that the devil specifically hates to hear are:

1. The name of Jesus

2. The references to the shed blood of Jesus on the cross

3. The quoted Word of God

The Power of the Name of Jesus Christ

On their way to the temple one day, Peter and John encountered a lame man who was asking for alms. This man had been lame from birth, and daily he was carried to the temple gate to beg for money. Peter said to him, "Silver and gold I do not have, but what I do have I give you: In the name of Jesus Christ of Nazareth, rise up and walk" (Acts 3:6). The Scriptures tell us that Peter then took the man by his right hand and lifted him up, and his feet and ankle bones received strength. He had never walked in his life, yet he was suddenly able to stand, walk, and leap about, all the while praising God.

Peter and John were doing what Jesus had told them to do. Jesus had said to His disciples on the night before His crucifixion, "Most assuredly, I say to you, whatever you ask the Father in My name He will give you. Until now you have asked nothing in My name. Ask, and you will receive, that your joy may be full" (John 16:23–24).

The name of Jesus is not something that we simply tack onto our prayers, however. Jesus gave to His disciples, including us, the "power of attorney" to use His name. When we pray "in the name of Jesus," we are praying as if Jesus Himself is praying. We are to pray what He would pray, asking for what He would request of our heavenly Father. A prayer that is truly in the name of Jesus is totally in line with God's Word and God's will.

The name of Jesus embodies all of the power and majesty that are rightfully Jesus' alone. His name is higher than any other name, and His power is greater than that of any person or any demon (Phil. 2:9–11). The name of Jesus is a constant reminder to the devil that he is not as powerful as Jesus. He does not have the relationship with the Father that Jesus has, nor is he the rightful heir to all of heaven. The devil doesn't want to be reminded of those truths.

Therefore God also has highly exalted Him and given Him the name which is above every name, that at the name of Jesus every knee should bow, of those in heaven, and of those on earth, and of those under the earth, and that every tongue should confess that Jesus Christ is Lord, to the glory of God the Father.

—Philippians 2:9–11

෴ What does it mean that the name of Jesus is "above every name"? If Jesus is Lord of all, what does this suggest about the devil's status?

෴ What does it say about the character of Jesus that every knee shall bow at the mere mention of His name?

The Power of the Shed Blood of Christ

When we pray, we enter into the throne room of God solely on the basis that Jesus Christ died for our sins. Throughout Scripture we find evidence that shed blood was the means God provided for His children to be reconciled to Himself and to one another. After Adam and Eve sinned in the Garden of Eden, God shed the blood of animals and made coats of animal skins for them to wear. These coats were a consistent reminder to them that God alone is the Giver, Author, and Ruler of all life (Gen. 3:21).

When the Israelites left Egypt for the promised land, God required them to put the shed blood of lambs on the doorposts of their homes. The death angel passed through Egypt, but it did not touch the homes where the blood had been applied. Again, God was making a provision for *life* through the shedding of blood (Ex. 12:12–13). God's Law required that animals be sacrificed. The shedding of blood was the means of reconciliation between God and people (Lev. 14:12–13).

The shed blood of Jesus on the cross was God's definitive act in providing forgiveness for all who would receive it. Jesus' death was the one final sacrifice for atonement. By His shed blood, Jesus purchased mankind's forgiveness from sin. Jesus said that His death was the "new covenant" and that His blood was "shed for many for the remission of sins" (Matt. 26:28).

In dying for our sins, Jesus dealt a mortal blow to the devil. That was His victory moment over Satan. No longer would Satan have access to Him to tempt Him. No longer would Satan have opportunity to keep Him from fulfilling God's purposes. Satan became a defeated foe the moment that Jesus died on the cross.

In the shed blood of Jesus, we have the means for forgiveness and eternal life. We also have protection against our adversary, who is the agent of destruction and death. When we engage in spiritual warfare against the devil, we are wise to pray, "By the authority of Jesus Christ and under the protection of His shed blood, I pray against Satan." The blood of Jesus is a terrible reminder to Satan that he lost his battle with Jesus and that he has no power over anything Jesus purchased with the price of His own blood.

> ...knowing that you were not redeemed with corruptible things, like silver or gold, from your aimless conduct received by tradition from your fathers, but with the precious blood of Christ, as of a lamb without blemish and without spot.
>
> —1 Peter 1:18–19

In what sense are silver and gold "corruptible things"? How is the blood of Christ incorruptible?

Why is it so important to understand that it was the blood of Christ that redeemed you? How does this fact give you power to defeat Satan?

The Power of the Quoted Word of God

The third thing the devil cannot stand to hear is the quoted Word of God. When we quote Scripture, we need to be very specific, just as Jesus was when He was tempted by Satan in the wilderness.

> Now when the tempter came to Him, he said, "If You are the Son of God, command that these stones become bread." But He answered and said, "It is written, 'Man shall not live by bread alone, but by every word that proceeds from the mouth of God.' " Then the devil took Him up into the holy city, set Him on the pinnacle of the temple, and said to Him, "If You are the Son of God, throw Yourself down. For it is written: 'He shall give His angels charge over you,' and, 'In their hands they shall bear you up, / Lest you dash your foot against a stone.' " Jesus said to him, "It is written again, 'You shall not tempt the LORD your God.' " Again, the devil took Him up on an exceedingly high mountain, and showed Him all the kingdoms of the world and their glory. And he said to Him, "All these things I will give You if You will fall down and worship me." Then Jesus said to him, "Away with you, Satan! For it is written, 'You shall worship the LORD your God, and Him only you shall serve.' " Then the devil left him, and behold, angels came and ministered to Him.

—Matthew 4:3–11

Each time the devil tempted Jesus, Jesus responded with the Word of God. He didn't rely on human opinion or a quote from a so-called expert. Nor did Jesus command the devil to do anything other than to depart from Him. Jesus quoted Scripture, and the power of the Scripture was sufficient in defeating Satan. If that method was good enough for Jesus, it should be good enough for you and me.

Note, too, that Jesus used Scriptures that related directly to each of Satan's temptations. He was very precise in His use of the Scriptures. A person must know the Bible if he wants to use it with precision. A Christian must be familiar with the truths of the Bible from cover to cover. Think of your Bible as being filled with live ammunition. The verses of the Bible are powerful weapons to use as you command the devil to depart from you. The Word of God indeed is your sword against your adversary (Eph. 6:17).

When quoting the Scriptures to the enemy, find a passage of the Bible that is directly related to the problem you are facing. Read that passage of Scripture aloud as part of your prayers, voicing your belief in God to act for good on your behalf.

> For the word of God is living and powerful, and sharper than any two-edged sword, piercing even to the division of soul and spirit, and of joints and marrow, and is a discerner of the thoughts and intents of the heart.
>
> —Hebrews 4:12

What does it mean that Scripture pierces "the division of soul and spirit, and of joints and marrow"?

๛ In what sense is the word of God living? In what ways is it fixed and unchanging?

Battling the Devil with Purity of Heart

When you speak the name of Jesus or quote the Word of God, you must do so with a pure heart that is totally submitted to the Lord Jesus Christ. The name of Jesus is not a magic word. The blood of Jesus is not a secret formula. We must never use the name of Jesus or make a reference to His blood in a cavalier or joking manner. Our battle with the enemy is deadly serious. Our position in Christ is the most important aspect of our lives. As Peter said:

> Be sober, be vigilant; because your adversary the devil walks about like a roaring lion, seeking whom he may devour.

> —1 Peter 5:8

๛ Why must we be vigilant against the devil? Why must we be sober when doing battle against him?

What weapons do we wield in that battle? What armor do we have?

Today and Tomorrow

TODAY: MY SOURCE OF POWER AGAINST THE DEVIL IS IN THE NAME OF JESUS AND HIS WORD.

TOMORROW: I WILL BEGIN A SCRIPTURE MEMORIZATION PLAN THIS WEEK.

LESSON 8

Saying No to Satan's World Order

----------- ❧ **In This Lesson** ☙ -----------

LEARNING: WHAT EXACTLY IS THE "WORLD ORDER"?

GROWING: HOW ARE THE WORLD'S PRIORITIES DIFFERENT FROM GOD'S PRIORITIES?

In recent years people have spoken about a new world order. They generally have been referring to the realignment of political power in the aftermath of the Soviet Union's collapse. The Bible speaks of a world order, but the word *new* is never applied to it. It is as old as humanity. In 1 John 2:15–17 we have a description of this world order:

> Do not love the world or the things in the world. If anyone loves the world, the love of the Father is not in him. For all that is in the world—the lust of the flesh, the lust of the eyes, and the pride of life—is not of the Father but is of the world. And the world is passing away, and the lust of it; but he who does the will of God abides forever.

A strong and related statement is found in 1 John 5:19:

> We know that we are of God, and the whole world lies under the sway of the wicked one.

The world order depicted in the Bible is not one in which Christians are to be involved. It is a world order established by our adversary. It is not eternal, but it is pervasive on the earth today. We must resist and counteract it every day of our lives. The good news is that we can! John holds out this hope:

> For whatever is born of God overcomes the world. And this is the victory that has overcome the world—our faith. Who is he who overcomes the world, but he who believes that Jesus is the Son of God?
>
> —1 John 5:4–5

Through Christ we have the wisdom and strength to live in a way that is opposed to Satan's world order.

What is "the World"?

The Bible uses the word *world* in three ways. First, it refers to the inhabited world, the sum of the nations. Jesus said, "Go into all the world and preach the gospel to every creature" (Mark 16:15). He was sending His disciples into all the inhabited regions and nations of the world.

Second, *world* is used to describe the whole of humanity. Jesus said, "For God so loved the world that He gave His only begotten Son, that whoever believes in Him should not perish but have everlasting life" (John 3:16). Jesus was referring to all the people of the earth.

Third, *world* is used to refer to a world system, or a world order. In Ephesians 2:1–2, Paul wrote, "And you He made alive, who were dead in trespasses and sins, in which you once walked according to the course of this world, according to the prince of the power of the air, the spirit who now works in the sons of disobedience." Paul was referring to the way the cosmos operates.

The word *world* is used 185 times in the New Testament, 105 of which occur in the writings of John. John spent most of his ministry in cities located on the west coast of Turkey, cities that at the time were heavily Greek in culture and Roman in rule. John was aware that the life of Jesus was 180-degrees opposed to the normal ways of Greek and Roman cultures.

ᕫ Cosmos ᕬ

The word *cosmos* refers literally to an arrangement of things. It is the key concept in understanding the devil's world order. The devil has a design, an "arrangement" that he desires to perpetuate upon humanity.

Every facet of life has an arrangement: politics, education, art, commerce, science, music, law. Each of these areas works in a particular way and functions under certain laws. These facets of life work together to create an even larger arrangement, a cosmos. The fact that things are arranged and ordered is not what is wrong; it is the way in which things are arranged that is the concern.

ᕫ The Perfect World Order ᕬ

The perfect world order is found in the first two chapters of Genesis. Adam was given the responsibility for governing a perfect world in a perfect way. In this perfect cosmos God was in charge, and Adam and Eve were completely reliant upon Him. They made only wise decisions because they trusted God to tell them what to do and how to do it. They enjoyed a perfect relationship with God and with one another—without manipulation, corruption, or sin. Their relationship mirrored perfectly the relationship they had with God.

❧ The Current World Order ❧

The perfect world order established by God in the garden of Eden collapsed when Adam sinned, and another world order was established. This world order included the influence of Satan and his ability to manipulate and control humanity. In this world order Satan sought to be the ruler of the earth, the one on whom mankind is reliant and the one to whom mankind turns for all decisions.

Every variety of world order since the demise of the garden of Eden has been structured on the same premise: Satan is seeking to be in absolute charge of all mankind. He desires to be the sovereign world ruler. Of course the natural laws of the earth, such as gravity, were established by God and cannot be violated without consequences that God also established. The unchanging laws of God include spiritual laws and laws related to the mind and emotions of mankind. However, the systems of this world—the organized power structures and the way they work—are largely under Satan's domain. As John said, "the whole world lies under the sway of the wicked one" (1 John 5:19).

God allows Satan's influence on the earth, but He also has placed a limitation on him. Jesus clearly stated that limitation:

> Now is the judgment of this world; now the ruler of this world will be cast out. And I, if I am lifted up from the earth, will draw all peoples to Myself.
>
> —John 12:31–32

Jesus was speaking of His ministry to heal the sick and the demon-possessed, as well as of His crucifixion on the cross. He was saying that those who believed in Him and accepted His sacrificial death on the cross would no longer be in the grip of Satan. They would be free to live in total obedience to God. They, therefore, need not live as victims of Satan's world order. They would still live *in* the world, but their behavior and attitudes would not be *of* the world (John 17:14–16).

> I have given them Your word; and the world has hated them because they are not of the world, just as I am not of the world. I do not pray that You should take them out of the world, but that You should keep them from the evil one. They are not of the world, just as I am not of the world.
>
> —John 17:14–16

✎ What did Jesus mean when He said that He was "not of the world"? What does it mean to be "of the world"? How does one avoid it?

✎ Why does God not remove Christians from the world once they are saved? What does He do instead?

Satan's Ploys

Satan uses two main ploys to draw men to himself so that they might live according to his design.

First, he makes his world order as attractive as possible. Satan does everything he can to make his world order highly appealing, but that attractiveness fades. Nothing that is held out by Satan can remain attractive. That's because everything Satan controls is seeded with Satan's own decay.

Second, he makes promises that he cannot keep. Every one of Satan's temptations is a promise of something that will be pleasurable, beneficial, and worthy of our participation. That promise is always short-lived. It cannot be fulfilled because it is not grounded in God's eternal goodness.

We must recognize Satan's purpose behind his ploys. Satan seeks our destruction, our demise, our death. His tricks are just that: tricks. He does not want us to flourish, prosper, or be blessed. All he offers is an *illusion* of goodness. The realities of his world order are deceit, confusion, pain, suffering, and despair.

We also must recognize that Satan is supremely self-centered. Everything he does is designed to magnify his self-serving power and his self-seeking glory. He isn't the least bit interested in sharing what he has amassed with anyone else. He is only interested in duping people to give him their souls. In the end everything that Satan holds out to mankind ends up being terrible.

Satan's Lies

Satan's world order is governed by three principal lies.

First, Satan says that man can be self-sufficient. Satan's foremost lie to mankind appeals directly to people's greatest fear—loss of control—and people's biggest character flaw—pride. Satan's lie is, "You don't need God. You can make it on your own." This is the lie he voiced to Eve in the garden of Eden. He said, "In the day you eat of it your eyes will be opened, and you will be like God, knowing good and evil" (Gen. 3:5).

God says, "You need a Source for your life. You are limited in power, wisdom, and ability. I am your Source. Furthermore, you were born with a sin nature, and you need a Savior. I have provided Jesus Christ to be your Savior."

> Now we have received, not the spirit of the world, but the Spirit who is from God, that we might know the things that have been freely given to us by God.
>
> —1 Corinthians 2:12

What things have been freely given to us by God? What things does the world offer?

❧ What is the spirit of the world? How does it differ from the Spirit of God?

Second, Satan says that the pursuit of pleasure is man's purpose on earth. Satan's lie is that if it feels good, we must acquire it or participate in it. From Satan's standpoint there are no illegitimate desires and all of man's lusts should be fulfilled. God says that our desires must be filled in righteous ways or we will suffer severe consequences.

> What comes out of a man, that defiles a man. For from within, out of the heart of men, proceed evil thoughts, adulteries, fornications, murders, thefts, covetousness, wickedness, deceit, lewdness, an evil eye, blasphemy, pride, foolishness. All these evil things come from within and defile a man.
>
> —Mark 7:20–23

❧ Define these sins in your own words:

Evil thoughts:

Lewdness:

An evil eye:

Foolishness:

～ Why does Jesus say that all these sins originate within our-selves?

Third, Satan says that security exists in possessions. Satan's lie is that people can purchase adequate defense, social status, and self-esteem. *Things* are exalted by Satan, as opposed to relationships. God's truth is that only God is our true defender, provider, and shield against evil. We come to a true sense of our worth when we realize that God sent His only Son to die in order that we might live. Any status we have, we have solely because God allows us to hold that position for the sake of His kingdom.

For what will it profit a man if he gains the whole world, and loses his own soul? Or what will a man give in exchange for his soul?

—Mark 8:36–37

How do the things of this world endanger your eternal soul? Give examples.

Priority on "Self" and "Now"

You'll note that each of Satan's lies places top priority on self and on the present. Satan does not want you to have a concern for other people or a concern for how your actions today might affect the future. Certainly we can look at our world today and see that people are primarily concerned with self, not God. Today's generation lives for today.

The three main lies of Satan are expressed by John as

1. the pride of life—mankind is completely self-sufficient.

2. the lust of the flesh—mankind's happiness and the fulfillment of all fleshly desires are supreme.

3. the lust of the eyes—mankind's position and security can be acquired by what man sees (1 John 2:16).

☙ Put each of the following into your own words and give examples of each:

Pride of life:

Lust of the flesh:

Lust of the eyes:

How to Live Free of Satan's World Order

Jesus offers us hope and assurance that we can be free of Satan's lies and live in truth. Truth is the key to staying out of the treachery of Satan's world order. God's commandments give us the most fruitful, beneficial, and blessed way to live. We live in truth and avoid Satan's world order when we know and obey God's statutes.

The truth of God is that Jesus Christ purchased our freedom from Satan through His death on the cross, and we can live in that freedom every day of our lives. We live in truth and avoid Satan's world order when we accept Jesus as our Savior and rely on Him daily to deliver us from evil.

The truth of God is that we do not need to be like this world. We can be transformed into the image of Christ Jesus. We live in truth and avoid Satan's world order when we ask the Holy Spirit to change our habits and our attitudes, and to make us more and more like Jesus.

> If you abide in My word, you are My disciples indeed. And you shall know the truth, and the truth shall make you free.

> —John 8:31–32

~ What does it mean to abide in God's Word? How is this done?

~ In what ways does God's truth set us free? What sorts of bondage do the lies of the world bring about?

Our Responsibility to Live Godly Lives

Our responsibility as Christians is not to live a life that has the world's approval. The Scriptures tell us that we are to live godly lives, regardless of the cost:

The grace of God that brings salvation has appeared to all men, teaching us that, denying ungodliness and worldly lusts, we should live soberly, righteously, and godly in the present age.

—Titus 2:11–12

As Christians, we will never have the approval of the world, and we waste our time if we try to win it. Rather than seek the approval of the world, we need to recognize that we are to be a light to the world, a bright witness to the truth of God's love and saving grace. Refuse to compromise with the world order that has been established by Satan. Refuse to participate in it. You are called to be a citizen of God's heavenly kingdom, which is an eternal, perfect order.

Therefore do not let sin reign in your mortal body, that you should obey it in its lusts. And do not present your members as instruments of unrighteousness to sin, but present yourselves to God as being alive from the dead, and your members as instruments of righteousness to God.

—Romans 6:12–13

What does it mean to let sin reign in your body? What rights does a reigning monarch have over his subjects?

Why are we commanded to present ourselves to God "as being alive from the dead"? What effect would death have on the lusts of our flesh?

 Today and Tomorrow

TODAY: THE LORD WANTS ME TO LIVE AS A LIGHT IN THIS WORLD, BRINGING GLORY TO HIM.

TOMORROW: I WILL ASK THE LORD TO SHOW ME AREAS WHERE WORLDLY THINKING HAS TAKEN ROOT IN MY MIND.

Facing the Spirit of Antichrist

❧ In This Lesson ❧

LEARNING: WHO IS THE ANTICHRIST?

GROWING: HOW CAN I RECOGNIZE THE LIES OF SATAN?

Throughout history greedy people have risen to power to promote their own personal causes. They nearly always couch themselves as the answer to a particular problem or even as the savior of the world. By the time these people reach a certain level of prominence and power, godly people have searched the Scriptures and concluded that they are not the Christ.

In some cases, the same godly people concluded that the leader in question was the Antichrist. So far, they have all been wrong. We have not yet experienced the presence of the Antichrist, for when he makes his appearance, the entire world will know his identity because he will loudly proclaim it.

A Person or a Spirit?

Is the Antichrist a person or a spirit? The answer is both. There will be a person whose doctrine and deeds will earn him the title of Antichrist. There also is a prevailing spirit of antichrist at work in our world today.

⤳ The Person Called Antichrist ⤶

The Antichrist will be a real man who will assume a right to rule the world and be the very embodiment of evil. He will be filled with and directed by Satan himself. In the book of Revelation John refers to this man as the Beast. He will manifest supernatural powers and exert global influence (Rev. 13).

⤳ The Spirit of Antichrist ⤶

The word *antichrist* appears only in the epistles of John. John's concern was far more with the *spirit* of antichrist, whom he regarded as Satan himself, than with the person who would one day be filled with Satan and dominate the world stage. John saw Christians as being in a real and present struggle with the devil, who seeks to be a false christ, a substitute, an "instead of" christ.

The prefix *anti* has two meanings. The first conveys the idea of *being in place of something*. The second conveys the idea of *being opposed to something*. Satan always seeks to be in place of Christ; he is always opposed to Christ. He is *anti*-Christ in everything that he says and does. He is the ultimate representation of ideas and behaviors opposed to Jesus. Many people have operated in the spirit of antichrist. This type of spirit is not a demon. Rather it is a philosophy, a mind-set, a way of thinking and behaving.

The Bible refers to several types of spirit. We each have a human spirit. Romans 8:16 tells us, "The Spirit Himself bears witness with our spirit that we are children of God." There is a spirit of the world as a whole, which is the prevailing philosophy of the world order we discussed in the last lesson. Paul wrote, "Now we have received, not the spirit of the world, but the Spirit who is from God, that we might know the things that have been freely given to us by God" (1 Cor. 2:12).

Paul and John also wrote about a pervasive spirit that characterizes evil people. In Ephesians 2:2 we read about the "prince of the power of the air, the spirit who now works in the sons of disobedience." John refers to "false prophets"—those who champion what is evil (1 John 4:1). Peter said, "There were also false prophets among the people, even as there will be false teachers among you, who will secretly bring in destructive heresies, even denying the Lord who bought them, and bring on themselves swift destruction" (2 Peter 2:1).

These people operate with an evil intent and speak things contrary to the will of God, and they are operating in the spirit of antichrist. Everything they say is opposed to Christ, and everything they do is an attempt to take over the place that is rightfully Christ's alone.

> But there were also false prophets among the people, even as there will be false teachers among you, who will secretly bring in destructive heresies, even denying the Lord who bought them, and bring on themselves swift destruction. And many will follow their destructive ways, because of whom the way of truth will be blasphemed.
>
> —2 Peter 2:1–2

✎ What "destructive heresies" have there been over the history of the Christian church? How have they denied the Lord (e.g., denied the deity of Christ)?

❧ How do false teachings blaspheme "the way of truth"?

Our Responsibility to Test the Spirits

Jesus warned His disciples that there would be people who would attempt to deceive the believers:

> Take heed that no one deceives you. For many will come in My name, saying, "I am the Christ," and will deceive many.... false christs and false prophets will rise and show great signs and wonders to deceive, if possible, even the elect.
>
> —Matthew 24:4–5, 24

Paul also warned against those who would preach any gospel other than the gospel of Christ. He spoke of "false apostles, deceitful workers, transforming themselves into apostles of Christ" (2 Cor. 11:13).

We are warned repeatedly throughout the Scriptures that we are never to accept a person's message as true on the basis of personality, appearance, or ability to communicate, or on the basis of the number of people who follow him, the music or testimonials he presents, or the promises he makes. The only basis of accepting any teaching must be this: is it in complete agreement with the written Word of God?

We are to *test* the spirits against the criterion of God's Word and specifically against the criterion of what is said about Jesus in God's Word. Any person who says that Jesus Christ is not God's Son come in the flesh, or who denies the sovereignty of Christ as the sole provision for salvation, is false (1 John 4:1–3).

We also must be on guard that we do not buy into a person's teaching or testimony because the person seems to be speaking the truth about one particular issue or concern. We must consider always the whole counsel of God's Word; *everything* a person says must be in line with God's Word, not just a portion of what he says.

> Beloved, do not believe every spirit, but test the spirits, whether they are of God; because many false prophets have gone out into the world.

> —1 John 4:1

What does it mean to "test the spirits"? How is this done in practical terms?

What criterion do we use to determine whether a teaching is of God or of the spirit of antichrist?

101

Characteristics of Those with False Spirits

Those who are filled with the spirit of antichrist, the devil's own spirit, often have the following characteristics:

1. They are manipulative. False teachers exploit others and use others for their own gain. If allowed to amass power, they will drain all of the finances of those who follow them. They destroy the individuality of their followers, often requiring that their followers dress and act in highly prescribed ways.

2. They promote sensuality. False teachers nearly always claim that sensuality is to be highly valued and sexual sins are permissible. Many cult leaders are advocates of blatant fornication and adultery.

3. They secretly introduce destructive heresies. They take a portion of God's Word and twist it into a form that seems reasonable to human desires. They hold out a principle about which men can say, "Yes, that's the way it *ought* to be." The trouble is, the principle that they proclaim is not what the Word of God holds to be truth. For example, false teachers today proclaim that there are many ways to approach God and experience salvation. People clamor after this heresy, saying, "Surely God wouldn't send a person to hell for not believing in Christ." The Bible says that Jesus is *the* way, *the* truth, *the* life, and that nobody comes to the Father but by Him (John 14:6).

4. They exhibit personal materialism and greed. False teachers with an antichrist spirit nearly always surround themselves with great wealth. Peter said, "By covetousness they will exploit you with deceptive words" (2 Peter 2:3).

The Outcome for Those with an Antichrist Spirit

The Scriptures give us a fivefold progression related to those who have an antichrist spirit. This progression is most evident in the life of the future antichrist world leader, called the Beast, but it is also the path that is followed by any person who allows himself to be filled with Satan's spirit.

First, the person displays lawlessness. The person with an antichrist spirit has no regard for God's law. To the contrary, he ridicules God's law as he dismisses its value. Those with an antichrist spirit also hold themselves to be above the laws that govern other people. They have little regard for order or justice. They rule according to their own whims and dictates. Paul wrote to the church at Thessalonica:

> The mystery of lawlessness is already at work; only He who now restrains will do so until He is taken out of the way.... The coming of the lawless one is according to the working of Satan, with all power, signs, and lying wonders.

> —2 Thessalonians 2:7, 9

Second, the person claims to be a deity. He claims special powers or wisdom, just as Satan before him. He claims to have knowledge about God that God hasn't revealed to others. At times the person will claim to be under God but on par with Jesus; the mindset is usually that Jesus was just a good man, a prophet, and that there have been many such people. False prophets claim that Jesus was only *a* son of God, not *the* Son, and that people today can have as much authority and dominion as Jesus. We are called to become sons of God and joint heirs with Christ, yet we are always under Christ's authority. The Bible never claims that any person can do what Christ did or be what Christ is: the only begotten Son of God, the Savior of the world, the Lord of lords and King of kings forevermore.

Paul addressed these lies directly: "There is no other God but one.... there is one God, the Father, of whom are all things, and we for Him; and one Lord Jesus Christ, through whom are all things, and through whom we live" (1 Cor. 8:4, 6).

Third, the person seeks to rule others. People who are filled with an antichrist spirit do not live in isolation. They recruit followers and build power structures. They long to manipulate, control, and rule over people. Their desire for power over other people is insatiable, although their outward demeanor may be one of false humility and gentleness.

Jesus taught us to pray to our heavenly Father, "Yours is the kingdom and the power and the glory forever" (Matt. 6:13). Anybody who attempts to get you to ascribe to his absolute rulership, power, and glory has an antichrist spirit.

Fourth, the person is a tool of Satan. The person may appear to be the one doing the ruling and teaching, but ultimately he is a pawn in the hands of Satan. Satan gives a form of power to his followers, but it is the power described in Revelation 9:3: "To them was given power, as the scorpions of the earth have power." This is the power to sting, to inflict pain, to cause suffering, to bring about loss, destruction, and devastation. Jesus taught, "Whoever commits sin is a slave of sin" (John 8:34). The person with an antichrist spirit may *think* that he is acting of his own accord; in reality he is a victim of Satan.

Fifth, the person is ultimately destroyed by God. God may allow a person with an antichrist spirit to exert influence for a season, but He will ultimately remove him from the scene. Paul wrote, "What fruit did you have then in the things of which you are now ashamed? For the end of those things is death.... the wages of sin is death, but the gift of God is eternal life in Christ Jesus our Lord" (Rom. 6:21, 23).

Nothing built by a person with an antichrist spirit survives for very long. False religions come and go. Cults rise and fall; empires crumble that were built by people with antichrist spirits. Only what is of Christ lasts on this earth. Only those whom Christ redeems will live forever.

> The coming of the lawless one is according to the working of Satan, with all power, signs, and lying wonders, and with all unrighteous deception among those who perish, because they did not receive the love of the truth, that they might be saved.
>
> —2 Thessalonians 2:9–10

What tactics does Satan use to deceive people into believing a lie?

According to these verses, why are people deceived? What must a person do to avoid being deceived into the lie of anti-christ?

Three Questions to Ask

If you believe you are facing a person who has a false spirit, there are three questions that you should ask him:

1. What do you believe about Jesus? Was He God? A person with an antichrist spirit will hem and haw at the question. The person who is a true Christian will say, "Jesus was God come in the flesh." John said, "Every spirit that does not confess that Jesus Christ has come in the flesh is not of God" (1 John 4:3).

2. What do you believe about mankind and about man's relationship to God? A person with an antichrist spirit will claim that mankind is supreme; God is a nice idea that is valuable to people, but in the end God is mankind's creation. Others with an antichrist spirit will claim that God exists to serve people. The true Christian will say, "Mankind is valuable to God, but he is always subservient to God. Mankind's role is to serve God."

A person with an antichrist spirit will claim that mankind has no need for salvation, and that if man desires to improve himself, he is capable of doing so without any help from God. The true Christian will say, "People need salvation and are incapable of achieving it on their own. Salvation is a gift of God, freely made available through Jesus Christ to all who will believe."

3. What do you believe about the Bible? A person with a spirit of antichrist will be opposed to hearing the Word of God and will have no interest in the things of God. He will dismiss the Bible's authenticity and authority. He will be opposed to any efforts to live a life in accordance with God's commandments.

The true Christian will say, "I believe the Bible to be the authoritative

Word of God, good for instruction. It presents the way that God wants me to live, think, feel, and believe."

When we ask these questions of a person, we must listen closely to the answers with spiritual ears. We must ask the Holy Spirit to alert us to anything that is contrary to God's Word. We can trust the Holy Spirit to prick our consciences so that we will be able to tell right from wrong. John said, "By this we know the spirit of truth and the spirit of error" (1 John 4:6).

> By this you know the Spirit of God: Every spirit that confesses that Jesus Christ has come in the flesh is of God, and every spirit that does not confess that Jesus Christ has come in the flesh is not of God. And this is the spirit of the Antichrist, which you have heard was coming, and is now already in the world.
>
> —1 John 4:2–3

What major heresies in history have claimed that Jesus did not "come in the flesh"? (For example, many groups deny that Jesus is God.)

Why would Satan work so hard to deny this truth?

Pervasive but Not Unbeatable

The spirit of antichrist is pervasive in our world today, but it can be confronted, challenged, and denied. We do not need to be victims of those who are operating according to Satan's dictates or who are filled with his spirit. We *can* overcome the enemy if we will be committed to a persistent, unrelenting obedience to God's truth.

✤ Today and Tomorrow ✤

TODAY: THE SPIRIT OF ANTICHRIST IS VERY ACTIVE IN THE WORLD TODAY.

TOMORROW: I WILL GUARD AGAINST SATAN'S LIES BY IMMERSING MYSELF IN GOD'S WORD.

LESSON 10

Choosing Faith over Reason and Emotion

┌───┐

─── ❧ **In This Lesson** ❧ ───

LEARNING: WHERE DO LOGIC AND EMOTIONS ENTER THIS BATTLE?

GROWING: WHAT IF I DON'T HAVE ENOUGH FAITH TO OBEY GOD?

└───┘

When faced with any decision in life, we operate from one of three positions: faith, reason, or emotion. Faith flows from the spirit of man. God endows us with faith so that we can make right choices related to Him. Reason and emotion flow from the soul of man, from what we often term the mind and the heart. Man experiences thoughts and feelings in his soul.

Thoughts and feelings are not eternal. They are related directly to the information, perceptions, and physical sensations that we have at a moment in time. Because of this, our thoughts and feelings can vary widely, according to time and circumstances. We often have competing thoughts and feelings, and we base them to a great extent on the thoughts and feelings of others who are close to us. Faith says in the face of a situation, "This is what God says." Reason says, "This is what I think and what seems right to me." Emotion says, "This is how I feel right now, and I am going to go with my feelings and do what feels good."

Faith, reason, and emotion are all related, of course. It's virtually impossible to separate them at times. But what we are concerned about in dealing with the devil is the fact that the devil never appeals to our faith. He only appeals to our reason and emotions. Furthermore, he attempts at all times to drive a wedge that separates faith from reason and emotions. When we honor and obey God in a situation, God works to bring our reason and emotions in line with our faith. When we obey the devil, we are fragmented and confused.

God Values Reason and Emotion

God is not opposed to reason or to our using our minds or expressing our feelings. Quite the contrary. God wants us to be reasonable and emotionally healthy people. God's laws are extremely reasonable and logical. When a person fully obeys God's laws, he experiences great joy.

What God desires is that we reason *with* Him, not apart from Him. In fact, the Scriptures tell us that He invites us to reason with Him: "Come now, and let us reason together" (Isa. 1:18). The very next verse describes the consequences to obedience and disobedience in this matter:

> If you are willing and obedient,
> You shall eat the good of the land;
> But if you refuse and rebel,
> You shall be devoured by the sword.

> —Isaiah 1:19–20

God wants us to understand that His thoughts, plans, and methods are greater than anything we could imagine:

> My thoughts are not your thoughts,
> Nor are your ways My ways....
> For as the heavens are higher than the earth,

So are My ways higher than your ways,
And My thoughts than your thoughts.

—Isaiah 55:8–9

No matter how much we know about a particular situation, we cannot know as much as God knows about it. As much as we might love another person and desire good on his behalf, we cannot love that person as much as God does. When we rely on our human emotions and reasoning ability, rather than submitting these to God and responding with our faith, we shortchange ourselves. And the devil delights anytime we deny God, ignore God, or fail to experience God's best.

How high above the earth is the very top of the universe? Why does God use this comparison to describe how His thoughts compare with your thoughts?

How do God's ways compare with your ways? How do God's methods differ from the methods of mankind?

The First Conflict Between Faith and Reason

We first see faith and reason in conflict in the garden of Eden. Satan took on the form of a beautiful and cunning serpent; then he came to Eve and said, "Has God indeed said, 'You shall not eat of every tree of the garden'?" And Eve replied, "We may eat the fruit of the trees of the garden; but of the fruit of the tree which is in the midst of the garden, God has said, 'You shall not eat it, nor shall you touch it, lest you die.'" The serpent told Eve, "You will not surely die. For God knows that in the day you eat of it your eyes will be opened, and you will be like God, knowing good and evil" (Gen. 3:1–5).

Satan appealed to Eve's reasoning ability. He introduced doubt: perhaps God didn't really mean what He had said, or perhaps God was holding out on Eve and not giving her everything that was for her good. Eve made a decision based on her reasoning ability, not on her faith in God. Throughout history we have continued to make Eve's mistake.

☙ When have you tried to use reason and logic to figure out God's will? What was the result?

☙ Eve had not been created yet when God told Adam not to eat the forbidden fruit. What doubts was the devil planting in her mind in this conversation?

Accepting and Obeying God's Absolutes

The world that Satan governs has no tolerance for God's absolutes. Consider these four issues:

- Prayer in schools

- Abortion policies

- Sexual identity

- Financial debt

In each of these areas people argue ardently from both reason and emotion. These highly volatile issues generate all manner of opinions and feelings in people. Answers, decisions, and public policies often are made on the basis of intellectual, logical reasoning. Individual decisions and attitudes very often are rooted in the way a person feels about the issue. People can argue all facets of these issues, and usually the more they argue their position, the more heated they become in their expression.

The alternative is to ask, "What does God say?" What does the Bible say about prayer? Is it good? Is it good for children? Is it appropriately applied to learning? What does the Bible say about taking innocent human life? What does the Bible say about bearing children and nurturing them according to godly principles? What does the Bible say about fornication, incest, and rape? What does the Bible say about homosexual behavior? What does the Bible say about borrowing and lending?

The biblical views on most issues of life are nearly always simple, straightforward, and easy to understand. God's commandments are not shrouded in mystery. Even a young child can understand the Ten

113

Commandments. The problem is not that we don't know God's opinion. The problem is that we don't want to obey what God says. Anytime that we know what to do and then fail to do it, we are in rebellion against God. That is a very dangerous position.

> The law of the LORD is perfect, converting the soul; the testimony of the LORD is sure, making wise the simple; the statutes of the LORD are right, rejoicing the heart; the commandment of the LORD is pure, enlightening the eyes; the fear of the LORD is clean, enduring forever; the judgments of the LORD are true and righteous altogether. More to be desired are they than gold, yea, than much fine gold; sweeter also than honey and the honeycomb. Moreover by them Your servant is warned, and in keeping them there is great reward.
>
> —Psalm 19:7–11

Put into your own words each quality of God's Word:

Perfect:

Sure:

Right:

Pure:

Clean:

True:

Faith Is the Only Way to Know God

When Paul wrote to the Corinthians, he was writing to Greeks who held reasoning and logic in very high regard. They were specialists in "the wisdom of man." The message of the Cross made no sense to them. Paul said to them:

> For the message of the cross is foolishness to those who are perishing, but to us who are being saved it is the power of God. For it is written: "I will destroy the wisdom of the wise, and bring to nothing the understanding of the prudent." Where is the wise? Where is the scribe? Where is the disputer of this age? Has not God made foolish the wisdom of this world? ... The foolishness of God is wiser than men, and the weakness of God is stronger than men.
>
> —1 Corinthians 1:18–20, 25

Reasoning is not the way we come to know God or to understand Him, because the human mind cannot comprehend God. All false religions assume otherwise. They believe that, if you only hone the intellect so that it is sharp enough, then you can analyze and understand God. They subject the intellect to a performance criterion.

Every false religious system or cult is based on performance, on meeting certain standards. A person is told what to do, for how long, and to what degree. None of it works because when you are facing an infinite, omniscient, omnipotent God, how can you possibly know when you have done enough, learned enough, or achieved enough? There is no way a finite creature can know the expectations of an infinite God.

Only by faith can we come to understand God—when we *believe* that God is just and righteous and merciful and loving and forgiving *solely* on the basis that this is what He said about Himself. Faith is believing that God has resources and evidence that we can't know. To a person who is attempting to find a logical way to God, the Cross is not going to make any sense at all. To the person who hopes to feel his way into God's presence, the Cross is going to be repulsive. And yet this is the means that God has chosen for the redemption of mankind. We must believe in God and believe that God knows best, not only for us but for every other person.

Why is the message of the cross "foolishness" in the world's eyes? Why does the world persistently reject Jesus' teachings that He is the only way to salvation?

≈ What is the "wisdom of this world"? How is it the opposite of God's Word?

God's Illogical Methods

God's laws and commandments are highly logical. God's methods very often are not. Consider these possibilities:

≈ An army commander is facing a major battle against a formidable foe, and he is told to have his troops circle a city once a day for six days and then circle it seven times on the seventh day, after which the troops are to blow trumpets and shout. The commander obeys and so do the troops. When the trumpets are sounded and the shouts are voiced, the walls of the city tumble and a victory is won.

≈ A leader is faced with a difficult situation. He has led thousands of people out into a wilderness area, but now they stand at the edge of an uncrossable sea. Approaching his people from the rear are the most powerful forces of Pharaoh, which are intent upon capturing the people and returning them to slavery. God tells the leader to put his rod into the water. He does so. The people walk across on dry ground.

≈ A young wife is facing a death sentence and opts to fast and pray, and then to host two dinner parties for her husband and her arch-enemy. In the course of the second dinnertime conversation, she openly accuses her enemy. In the end her own life is spared, along with the lives of her people.

☙ Three young leaders are told that they must bow to a statue that has been built by the emperor. They are told that, if they refuse, they will be thrown into a fiery furnace. They refuse, nonetheless, and God allows them to be thrown into the furnace. They live through the experience, coming out of the furnace without even the smell of smoke on their clothes.

Do any of these situations make any intellectual sense? No! They are contrary to logic and reasoning. Do any of these situations make sense in light of normal emotional responses? No! The normal emotional response would be to cave in to fear and seek an alternative plan.

By faith, however, Joshua, Moses, Esther, Shadrach, Meshach, and Abed–Nego scored mighty victories that brought glory to God. What God asked them to do was highly illogical and against normal human emotional response: march around a city and shout, put a rod into the water, prepare a couple of banquets, and be thrown into a fiery furnace. Actions based solely on faith, however, brought about good results for God's people and the elimination of God's enemies.

> Jesus said to him, "If you can believe, all things are possible to him who believes." Immediately the father of the child cried out and said with tears, "Lord, I believe; help my unbelief!"
>
> —Mark 9:23–24

☙ Read the full story of this demon-possessed boy in Mark 9:17–27. How did Jesus' methods differ from the world's methods in dealing with the sick boy?

☙ Explain the paradox of the father's words: "I believe; help my unbelief". How does God help us when our faith is weak?

Refuse to Be Blinded

When we understand God through reason alone, our reasoning efforts blind us to God. Paul wrote:

> If our gospel is veiled, it is veiled to those who are perishing, whose minds the god of this age has blinded, who do not believe, lest the light of the gospel of the glory of Christ, who is the image of God, should shine on them.

> —2 Corinthians 4:3–4

As long as we demand that logic be followed, we cannot accept much of the Bible, for it simply does not make sense to us. Nobody can pull this blindfold from our eyes. Each of us must come to the conclusion for ourselves: "Lord, I believe, help my unbelief." We are incapable of seeing the fullness of God's truth until we take this first step.

☙ Who is "the god of this age"? How does he blind the minds of people today? Give examples.

⟡ What is the world's motive for inventing false religions, according to the verses above?

No Excuses

The devil continually tempts us to justify our sins and to reason away our faith. He constantly entices us to respond to our emotions—especially fear, anger, and hatred—rather than to respond with faith. Don't listen to him! Choose to respond with your faith. When you respond with faith in Jesus Christ, you put your adversary on the run.

Join the Battle

The very mention of the devil's name evokes fear in many people. For others, the devil seems to be a joke. As Christians, we are to take the devil seriously, but we are not to be overwhelmed by him or give in to his temptations. We are not to ignore him or dismiss him lightly, but rather, we are to face him, resist him, and use our faith to overcome him.

We can take this stance only if we remain close to Christ Jesus, turn to the Holy Spirit daily for wisdom, courage, and direction, and above all, choose to believe what Christ has said to us: we *are* God's forgiven children, and the devil has no claim on our eternal spirits.

Others may pray for us, believe with us, and encourage us in our battle against the enemy—all to our benefit—but in the end we cannot hide behind the faith of others. Facing the devil is something each of us must do if we are to grow in our relationship with God. Facing the devil exercises our personal faith. It is an act of personal obedience to God. We must be *willing* to face the enemy of our souls if we are to be in a position to receive all the blessings and rewards that God has for us.

In Christ Jesus you *can* and *will* overcome the enemy. Engage in the battle. Trust God today for a victorious life!

❧ Today and Tomorrow ☙

TODAY: THE ONLY WAY TO FULLY KNOW GOD IS THROUGH FAITH.

TOMORROW: I WILL ASK THE LORD TO STRENGTHEN MY FAITH THROUGH HIS WORD AND HOLY SPIRIT.

❧ Notes and Prayer Requests: ❧

❧ Notes and Prayer Requests: ❧

The Life Principles Series

STUDY GUIDES

Other Books by Charles Stanley